Man often becomes what he believes himself to be. If I keep on saying to myself that I cannot do a certain thing, it is possible that I may end by really becoming incapable of doing it. On the contrary, if I have the belief that I can do it, I shall surely acquire the capacity to do it even if I may not have it at the beginning.

Mahatma Gandhi

This book is dedicated to those who have been courageous enough to develop the belief that they can do it and to the numerous and varied practitioners that have supported their endeavour.

Contents

Figures

Meet the author

Phil Musson's career in social work has been one of continual development from student to skilled practitioner to training officer to senior lecturer. He readily acknowledges that social work is a demanding occupation at both emotional and intellectual levels. He also acknowledges a sense of privilege in having spent the majority of his working life as a social worker and latterly as a facilitator in the learning and development of others who are or wish to also become qualified social work practitioners. It is, he believes, incumbent on the practitioner to have a conscious and deliberate understanding of why and how they intervene in the lives of their service users and he hopes this book will make a valued contribution towards that understanding.

Foreword

We are curious beings, always wanting to know the whys and wherefores of this and that. We ask why things behave one way rather than another. We wonder why people do what they do. The need to make sense drives us to reflect, think and come up with ideas, to have theories. The field of human development and individual behaviour, social interaction and personal relationships is a particularly complex and messy bit of the world of which to make sense. It is also the bit which we have to understand if we are to have any chance of getting by, personally and professionally. However, being so busy and tangled, making sense of the social world is not always easy or straightforward. This is why the social and psychological sciences have generated so many different theories, each trying to make sense of human development, individual behaviour and social interaction. And to make matters worse, these many theories often don't agree with one another. Disputes and debates have been rife ever since men and women first asked questions such as: How should we raise our children? How should we behave? What is a good life? How should we live together? Social workers, of course, find themselves grappling with the muddle of the human condition on a daily basis. This is why the profession is awash with a bewildering array of theories.

However, the old adage that there is nothing so practical as a good theory remains true. And if social life, particularly the slice with which social workers find themselves dealing, is so complicated, then it should come as no surprise that the profession finds itself with so many theories as it tries to make sense of individuals, their relationships and the society in which they live. This is why social work practice stimulates as much as it challenges, rewards as much as it frustrates. Even so, we need help if we are to navigate our way through and around the crowded curriculum of theories and their methods. And happily, a new guiding hand now comes along in the form of Phil Musson and his book, *Making Sense of Theory and its Application to Social Work Practice*. Phil takes us on a personal journey as he introduces and explains, applies and evaluates many of the major theories and approaches that currently populate social work practice. One of the neat, clarifying devices he uses to help the reader understand and take stock of each theory, is to apply each one, in turn, to the same case – the case of Annette and her family – to see what that particular theory has to say about what is going on, why it might be happening, and what might be done about it. The recognition that social workers have to deal with situations that are generally fuzzy, shifting and dynamic is thoughtfully handled. As each theory is used to look at Annette and her circumstances, so the focus of interest changes and the angle of understanding shifts.

The author encourages the reader to be open-minded. In recognising that complexity and uncertainty characterise many of the cases held by social workers, Phil Musson believes that taking a rounded approach is likely to be more effective and ethically sound. The result is an easy-to-read, compact and smartly ordered review of the profession's theories and their application.

David Howe
Emeritus Professor of Social Work
University of East Anglia, Norwich

Acknowledgements

I would like to thank my colleagues Sally Riggall and Jimmy Osbourne – Sally for her invaluable comments on my draft and Jimmy for his patience in introducing me to clipart. I would also like to mention Tracey Newby who is our social work subject librarian here at the University of Lincoln and I would like to express my thanks for her support with referencing.

Finally I would like to thank those service users, fellow practitioners, academic colleagues and students who I have had the privilege to work with and who have contributed so much to my learning.

Introduction

Welcome to this book on theories, approaches and their methods of intervention. The theories introduced and discussed in the book have the property of offering an explanation for our behaviour; they have a stab at answering the question, *what's going on?* The approaches introduced and discussed in this book do not have this property but are underpinned by a theoretical proposition which gives them their identity and validates the contribution they make. The methods of intervention introduced and discussed in this book are associated with the theory or approach that gives rise to them. A case study is applied to each method of intervention. The same case study is used so the reader can see how it is applied and form a view as to its efficacy.

In the late 1980s I was a student social worker on placement in a local authority's area office and I was struck by the differing volume of the files in the slings in the filing cabinets. In addition to basic information and some pro formas, the files held records of the intervention that families were receiving or had received. Different families have different needs and to an extent this may have explained why some families' files were slim and others' bulkier. However, some families had files that occupied more than one sling; some several. The files of a few families were so numerous that they occupied whole drawers of filing cabinets, cataloguing multi-generational intervention and often describing a panoply of involvement from the offer of support to contested legal proceedings. I tried to explain this and perhaps somewhat simplistically came up with three options:

Social work intervention in its current form 'works' intermittently.

The skills of social workers is varied and this results in different outcomes.

Change for some families is too big an ask.

You will be relieved to know that I have since developed a somewhat more sophisticated analysis of what might be going on but I cannot claim to have left these questions behind altogether. At the time I determined to try to optimise my skills in the service of those I would have the opportunity to work with and this book is related to that commitment.

It could be said that sensible people learn from experience but there have been occasions where sense has, for a myriad of reasons, evaded us or more accurately we have evaded sense. Sometimes we can *see* sense for ourselves but where it evades us but not, allegedly, others, there is the additional complication of whose sense we are seeing or are expected to see. Our capacity for doing so is something that has kept playwrights and philosophers busy for millennia and will doubtless continue to do so. As a species we span an impressive range of capability from a primate on the savannah to contemplating the shape and size of the universe and we can exhibit corresponding behaviours.

Change involves becoming pioneers – exploring terrain unfamiliar to us. Successfully incorporating change involves inhabiting the 'new' terrain, voluntarily losing the one we know. It is easy to see why it is a big ask.

This book is a modest review of the prevalent ideas that drive our behaviour and approaches that influence it. I hope you enjoy reading it and that it makes a valued contribution to your understanding and practice.

Phil Musson

February 2017

Why apply social science theory to social work practice?

Implicit in any social work interaction between a practitioner and the service user, be that an individual, group or community, is the premise that a social work service is required and that the social worker will provide it. On the face of it this is tantamount to an act of trust. In order for society to function a number of things are assumed: these include certain roles, responsibilities and capabilities. A range of structures are put in place, many of which are legitimately discriminatory in order for us to have confidence in the service which we are receiving. In respect of social work, these include selection processes (students and staff), assessment, qualifications and training, quality assurance and inspection processes, vetting and barring checks, registration and the requirements for its renewal.

Global definition of the social work profession

The international definition of social work was approved by the IFSW General Meeting and the IASSW General Assembly in July 2014:

Social work is a practice-based profession and an academic discipline that promotes social change and development, social cohesion, and the empowerment and liberation of people. Principles of social justice, human rights, collective responsibility and respect for diversities are central to social work. Underpinned by theories of social work, social sciences, humanities and indigenous knowledge, social work engages people and structures to address life challenges and enhance wellbeing.

(IFSW, 2014)

Given this definition of social work, it follows that the understanding and application of theory derived from social science is a requirement of social work education, training and practice. In the College of Social Work's *Professional Capabilities Framework* (currently minded by BASW, 2015), against which student social workers are assessed, capability 5 (*Knowledge: Apply knowledge of social sciences, law and social work practice theory*) specifically indicates:

> » Apply knowledge from a range of theories and models for social work intervention with individuals, families, groups and communities, and the methods derived from them.

The Department for Education's *Knowledge and Skills Statement for Approved Child and Family Practitioners* (2015) makes specific reference to the need to '*test multiple hypotheses about what is happening within families and identify which methods will be of help*'.

So the first answer to the question, *Why apply social science theory to social work practice?* is because it is a professional requirement.

This requirement has a rationale. How else could a practitioner approach the task of making sense of what's going on? Of making an assessment? Of developing a cogent analysis of the information gathered? Of using this to inform a plan of intervention?

All social work intervention seeks essentially to establish two things:

1. What is going on?

2. What are we going to do about it?

The second objective is contingent on coming to an informed decision in answer to the first. Coming to a decision about the first objective may involve some degree of speculation but if it is to be an informed decision the amount of speculation should be minimal. The application of theory, derived from social science, makes a valuable contribution in assisting the social worker to come to an informed decision regarding *what's going on* and it is only when this is established that a plan of intervention can be made, tailored to address the issues identified to be *going on*. It follows that if the assessment of *what's going on* is inaccurate or missing significant factors, or simply wrong, then the *what are we going to do about it?* part, however detailed a plan of intervention it might be, is likely to be ineffective. The promotion of effective intervention is the second reason why theory from the social sciences should be applied to social work practice. Anything less than the application of social science theory to social work practice would result in guesswork – a hunch or a shot in the dark.

Social workers are required to be accountable for, and be able to substantiate, their practice where called upon to do so. Furthermore, through changes resulting from the Children and Families Act 2014, in court proceedings there is less reliance on the evidence of 'expert witnesses' and more on that of social workers who are increasingly becoming to be seen as such. The practitioner is much more likely to be granted the order they have applied for and have an easier time in the witness box if they can give the rationale for the course their intervention has taken, going beyond description to cogent analysis, drawing on theory and an evidence base. So the third answer to the question is to demonstrate accountability and professional integrity.

The ethics of applying social science theory to social work practice

It is also a requirement of professional social work practice for practitioners to have knowledge of and apply ethics and values appropriately. Social workers are rightly sensitive to power dynamics between themselves and their service users. This, again rightly, extends to considerations of dress, demeanour and the manner in which they discharge their 'expert' power. The last few decades has seen the development and growing influence of practice which seeks to: empower the service user; work with them in a spirit of partnership, collaboration and co-operation; work with greater equality, giving recognition to their 'expertise'; and work from a model of exchange (Smale et al, 2000, p 140). These approaches are discussed in greater detail in Chapter 3 but the developments were welcomed by practitioners as they, quite rightly, felt more 'in tune' with the value of working *with* service users. However, these developments should not detract from the practitioner's preparedness to apply the full range of theory, approach and the respective methods of intervention available to them. Some serious case reviews, for example that of Daniel Pelka (Lock, 2013), have made the rather unhelpful recommendation to '*think the unthinkable*', which is a contradiction in terms. Practitioners are required to think and this includes as full a panoply of explanations for what they see as their expertise permits.

Practitioners have a Kantian duty to provide their service users with the best service they can offer. In the case of Daniel, this did not solely extend to his welfare. Had the practitioners involved realised what was happening to Daniel, and had worked out *what was going on*, they may have: saved his life and the additional trauma suffered by him; prevented long-term jail sentences for his mother and partner; the death of his mother in prison; and any guilt his sister felt at being required to be complicit in his abuse by 'covering up' the real causes of his injuries. The *best service* was owed to Daniel, his immediate family, the extended family, the agencies who employed the practitioners and society in order for its members to have confidence in its public services.

Expectations of theoretical explanation

In November 2014, the European Space Agency's spacecraft Rosetta released its probe *Philae*, which successfully landed on Comet 67P. This was ten years after launch, a journey of 6.4 billion kilometres travelling at times of up to 775 metres per second.

The probe sent pictures of the comet and other data back to Earth, a distance of 510 million kilometres.

On 1 January 2017, a man dressed as Santa Claus shot dead 39 people in a nightclub in Istanbul. The victims were comprised of many different nationalities who were 'seeing in' and celebrating the New Year.

These two seemingly unrelated events illustrate an important contrast in human achievement. The first is an astonishing example of what human ingenuity in engineering and the understanding of the physical laws of maths and physics can achieve. The second is a lamentable expression of our failure as human beings to achieve peaceful coexistence. Why might this be? The physical laws appear fixed. They don't have individual agency through which to encounter life and develop a resulting interpretation on what this means for them. We may wish human behaviour was as predictable as the principles that govern the laws of nature appear to be but this is not the case. Indeed, it if was, it should be possible to write a biological/electrical/organic equation that could describe this thought. Such an equation is currently beyond our understanding; perhaps it will remain so but it is instructive about the extent to which we may be confident about understanding and predicting human behaviour. Therefore, in the taxonomy of certainty, *theory* may be thought of as an informed, organised, systematised construct of what is going on. It may have an evidence base but so might contrary explanations. This is a significant improvement on a construction that is not informed and lacks a systemised approach and rational organisation, as this would be a guess, but *social* science cannot claim to have exposed the laws and principles *physical* science has been able to do.

This does not diminish or detract from the endeavour of trying to come to an understanding of what drives behaviour, provided it is accepted that such an enquiry is theorising. Such theorising provides the practitioner with a framework with which to approach social phenomena in a structured way from which a plan of intervention

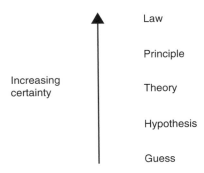

Figure 1.1 The taxonomy of uncertainty

may be devised. From the theories and approaches discussed in this book, practitioners may have ones they prefer to others; the student may develop such preferences. A reflective practitioner would have an awareness of the reasons for such preferences. The practitioner can expect a theory to offer a proposal that goes some way to explain the social phenomena. The proponent may claim more of their theory but it cannot be regarded as a complete explanation as this would merit being described as a law. It is for the practitioner to determine the extent to which the theory in question offers them a satisfactory explanation for what they are seeing, which may be the basis upon which preferences may be built.

Unhelpful ideas

As a social work academic, I encourage students and practitioners to embrace all ideas within the profession's knowledge base and subject them to their own critical analysis as to how helpful or otherwise they find them in making a useful contribution to aiding their understanding. As a practitioner I have undertaken this process and I offer the following thoughts on concepts and ideas that I have found unhelpful in making a useful contribution to aiding my understanding. I have limited these to two for reasons of brevity, but have selected these on the basis of the influence they appear to have amassed. These thoughts are offered simply for the readers' consideration and should be subject to the assertion in the first sentence of this paragraph.

The first unhelpful idea is:

Dualism

There may be sound reasons in philosophical debate for dividing phenomena into one of two expressions, mind and body, for example. However, in coming to an understanding of what is going on, attempting that worthy, if ambitious, quest of determining a more accurate representation of reality, I find it deeply unhelpful. The proposition that a phenomenon is either one thing or another rarely seems to be borne out. We speak of black and white as opposing elements but we know 'white' light to be comprised of several colours, that these are differentiated by their wavelength and our recognition of them is determined by which of them are absorbed and which reflected.

Human development has been subject to a dualistic analysis in so far as it is determined by nature *or* nurture. Protagonists of one or the other of these explanations have even spoken of nature *versus* nurture as if one could be conceived and brought up either with a biology and no environment or an environment and no biology. Is it not apparent that one is an inextricable compound of the two? In coming to an assessment of a child with special educational needs, any congenital condition would need to be considered, as would the degree of stimulation the environment provided.

The unquestioning adoption of a dualistic analysis can restrict options for practitioners and in consequence can result in a disservice for service users. For example: Within the *caring professions* there seems to be an ongoing debate about the relative merits of a medical model *or* a social model of analysis. As professions tend to align themselves to a greater extent with their area of expertise and values, it follows that nurses will be inclined to a medical body of knowledge and social workers to a social one. This is of course perfectly reasonable but a problem can occur when one undermines or seeks to be dismissive of the others' *body of knowledge* or *model* the profession is predominantly aligned to.

The case study the theories, approaches and their methods of intervention are applied to in this book involves a young woman whose name is Annette. You will be introduced to Annette and her circumstances but two presenting issues are that she may be depressed and she is overweight. These of course may be interrelated; however, in seeking to better understand what's going on and what (if anything) may be done about it, the eclectic practitioner might consider the usefulness of short-term medication and the possibility of an underactive thyroid as well as the pressures she has, the sources of support she has access to and her lifestyle choices in terms of diet and exercise.

The eclectic practitioner gives recognition to what other models (to their own) 'bring to the table' in helping the service user.

The second unhelpful idea is:

Post-modernism as a viable theoretical approach to social work practice

In order to evaluate a critique of post-modernism, an understanding of modernism is required. Modernism is a concept derived from the Enlightenment, a period characterised by rapid intellectual and scientific development that took place in the UK and parts of Europe throughout the mid-eighteenth and nineteenth centuries, a product of which was the industrial revolution of that time. Prior to this period, the causes of phenomena and events, such as the plague in the mid-seventeenth century which decimated the UK's population, were put down to religiously inspired wrath or superstition; there was no alternative explanation.

Joseph Wright of Derby painted *An Experiment on a Bird in the Air Pump* in 1768 and captured the dawning of the age of the Enlightenment. See www.nationalgallery. org.uk/paintings/joseph-wright-of-derby-an-experiment-on-a-bird-in-the-air-pump.

The painting depicts a family gathering, who for their own entertainment are carrying out an experiment in which air is pumped out of the bell jar, causing the dove, entrapped within, to falter and flop down as though dead but is revived when air is pumped back in, provided it is done soon enough. They did not understand what was actually happening; oxygen was not discovered until 1774 and its association with haemoglobin and circulation were not understood until later but this picture captures an instant on the cusp of discovery, the eve of understanding.

Modernism holds that phenomena and events *are* fathomable provided the knowledge by which to explain them is available. Although this is subject to a continuum over time, the notion of progress was set in train. We (the human race) can aspire to and achieve progress in medicine, technology and social well-being through the pursuit, acquisition and application of knowledge, achieved through scientific and intellectual enquiry.

Post-modernism critiques modernism and holds that any sense of objective reality or truth is illusionary and that human experience is confined to relativism, fragmentation and one's perception or interpretation. Of course, this dualistic analysis suffers from the problem discussed in the previous section; that of complex ideas being straightjacketed into two oppositional camps. But the inevitable conclusion for post-modernists is that anything beyond the individual is unattainable and so, by extension, are the *grand narratives* of analysis and progress.

At its simplest, a modernist would consider that we, as humans, have more in common with each other than what is different whereas the post-modernist would assert the opposite. Perhaps these diametrically opposed positions are not the best representation of reality. Consider an orchestra playing a popular piece of classical music.

The orchestra is Barenboim's West-Eastern Divan Orchestra, its musicians a mix of Arab and Israeli and other nationalities; despite having diverse languages, cultures and religions they have learnt one language in common that enables them to recreate the symphony intended by the composer despite him being long since dead. The audience are mixed in gender, predominantly older rather than young. A few are moved to tears in one movement but this is the adagio characterised by minor chords. The humans in the auditorium, musicians and audience, have their biology: their physiology and psychology in common but might also have some thoughts, feelings and experiences in common as well as those unique to them. Perhaps drilling down into the sheer complexity of an occasion such as the concert provides for a better representation of its reality?

Social work emerged from and is a product of the modernist tradition. Returning from sea-faring in 1720, Thomas Coram looked at the poor, destitute and discarded babies and infants of London; he thought: *We can and should do something about this* and founded the Thomas Coram Foundling Hospital. He was not alone. J F Handel organised fund-raising concerts and Hogarth brought public attention to the plight of the dispossessed drink dependents through his artwork, *Gin Lane* (1751).

Social work seeks to make a collective statement to the effect that there are standards of care and welfare, below which should not be tolerated or experienced. That is about as modernist an idea as is possible to assert and the reason why, in my opinion, post-modernism as a viable theoretical approach to social work practice is an unhelpful one. However, I am not alone in this assertion. Malcolm Payne, in his book *Modern Social Work Theory*, states '*Social work is a product of modernism*' and continues: '*because it is based on the idea that we can understand and study social problems and societies and take rational action to deal with the problems we see*' (Payne, 2005, p 15). Such an assertion may become mediated by what we choose to prioritise but this does not invalidate the assertion. Neil Thompson, in his book, *Theorizing Social Work Practice*, states: '*I believe it (post-modernism) should be rejected as a theoretical underpinning for social work*'. He supports this by asserting that '*post-modernism rejects the scientific notion of progress*' (Thompson, 2010, p 25). He dedicates Chapter 2 of his book to the topic as testament to it being worth detailed exploration.

Post-modernism has a contribution to make in offering a critique about the validity of knowledge. However, this is not a new criticism. Enquiry itself and most knowledge-bearing times and events have a context, a construction, but this doesn't render the knowledge any more false than it does true. These properties should be ascribed based on the application of the scientific method. This is more difficult within social science due to ethical considerations and the number of variables. Nevertheless, having a healthy scepticism towards information that is presented as knowledge is not a post-modernist stance but a characteristic of intelligence.

A comment on anti-oppressive and anti-discriminatory practice

I am not suggesting for a minute that these concepts are unhelpful, but when they are trotted out, mantra-like, as a pillar of social work practice without reference to the contested field in which social work takes place, this is unhelpful. You cannot uphold the rights of one person without (potentially) oppressing and discriminating against another. This may be legally and morally justified but may also attract social censure. It fell to a social worker to undertake a parenting assessment of the mother of Peter Connelly to determine if she could be entrusted to raise a child of a subsequent pregnancy. It falls to a social worker to monitor an elderly person living in the community who is neglectful of their self-care but has capacity. It falls to a social worker to intervene if that elderly person is being neglected by their carer; or to place an unaccompanied asylum-seeking young person who claims to be under 18 in foster care; to protect a young person at risk of sexual exploitation ostensibly against their wishes; to protect a child or young person from abuse or the practice of female genital mutilation or enforced marriage and other 'cultural' practices that some consider appropriate. Many situations in which social work takes place are complex and rarely without dilemma in which pathway has to be taken through competing rights, needs and responsibilities. Social work practice is not served well by failing to acknowledge this from the outset.

Theories of explanation and approaches and their respective methods of intervention

This book will introduce and offer comment on four theories of explanation and their respective methods of intervention, and four approaches and their respective methods of intervention. A case study will be used to show how each method of intervention could be applied to social work practice.

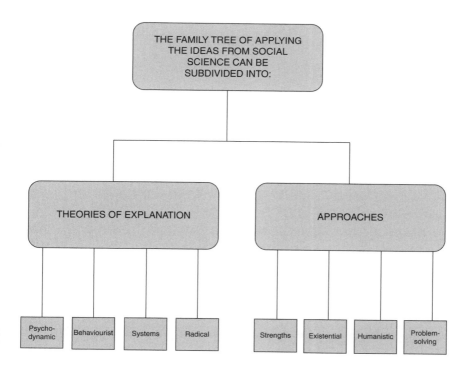

References

British Association of Social Workers (BASW) (2015) *Professional Capabilities Framework*. Birmingham: BASW. [online] Available at: www.basw.co.uk/pcf/ (accessed 18 March 2017).

Children and Families Act 2014 (c.6) (2014) London: TSO. [online] Available at: www.legislation.gov.uk/ukpga/2014/6/contents/enacted (accessed 18 March 2017).

Department for Education (2015) *Knowledge and Skills Statements for Child and Family Social Work*. Manchester: Department for Education. [online] Available at: www.gov.uk/government/publications/knowledge-and-skills-statements-for-child-and-family-social-work (accessed 18 March 2017).

Hogarth, W (1751) *Gin Lane*. London: Tate. [online] Available at: www.tate.org.uk/art/artworks/hogarth-gin-lane-t01799 (accessed 18 March 2017).

International Federation of Social Workers (IFSW) (2014) Global definition of social work. Berne, Switzerland: IFSW. [online] Available at: http://ifsw.org/get-involved/global-definition-of-social-work/ (accessed 18 March 2017).

Lock, R (2013) *Serious Case Review Re Daniel Pelka*. Coventry: Coventry Safeguarding Children Board. [online] Available at: https://library.nspcc.org.uk/HeritageScripts/Hapi.dll/filetransfer/2013CoventryDanielPelkaOverview.pdf?CookieCheck=42763.8944195255&filename=CC18C70DB7C8C3D49403BB94EB176F95207E5F66235DCA89651F5ED2BA5DA9311A353B626FC11241A3DF9A45C446BB4D1ABAD0-4545542F86BCD0195126CC3B3355977BB90D159C20EA09AB8B2D2C41A1697DB46FA6C272BFE0D17EA0326BD71411D0E7CA&DataSetName=LIVEDATA (accessed 18 March 2017).

Payne, M (2005) *Modern Social Work Theory* (3rd ed). Basingstoke: Palgrave Macmillan.

Smale, G, Tuson, G, Staham, D and Campling, J (2000) *Social Work and Social Problems: Working towards Social Inclusion and Social Change*. London: Palgrave Macmillan.

Thompson, N (2010) *Theorizing Social Work Practice*. Basingstoke: Palgrave Macmillan.

Wright, J (1768) *An Experiment on a Bird in the Air Pump*. London: National Gallery. [online] Available at: www.nationalgallery.org.uk/paintings/joseph-wright-of-derby-an-experiment-on-a-bird-in-the-air-pump (accessed 18 March 2017).

Chapter 2

What's going on? Theories of explanation and their application to social work practice

LEARNING OUTCOMES

By the end of this chapter you should understand the rudiments of psycho-dynamic, behavioural, systems and radical theories of explanation and see how they are applied to a case study.

The case study used will be essentially the same, with minor changes for the purposes of emphasis only. By using the same case study, the differences in the ways we can interpret *what's going on* and the consequential method of intervention employed can be compared more easily than if different case studies were used.

You are invited to consider the extent to which each of the four theories provides an explanation of the social phenomena described in the case study.

For reasons explored in Chapter 1, in the section 'Expectations of theoretical explanation', no one theory is likely to provide a wholly satisfactory explanation of *what's going on* but it is likely that it can make a useful contribution towards such an understanding. However, due to the nature of social phenomena and our limited understanding of their mechanics, the proportion by which each theory can be said to accurately 'explain' *what's going on* is restricted to conjecture. The proportion *you* might ascribe to any one will depend on your personal preference. This is comprised of a number of factors and could include: the extent to which it makes sense in relation to your own experience, your world view, political leanings, values, training and education and what you feel comfortable working with. Working in such a varied landscape does not detract from the need for the social worker to come to an informed 'take' on *what's going on* as doing so is an essential task of any proposed assessment and intervention.

PSYCHO-DYNAMIC THEORY

Headlines

It's all about the mechanics of the mind

Past experience influences, if not produces, personality

Development is in stages, 'success' in traversing a stage is influenced by the degree of anxiety the transition provokes; if/how this is resolved and the quality of transitions in previous stages.

'Therapy' requires a clinician to unpick this as it is not 'accessible' to the individual concerned.

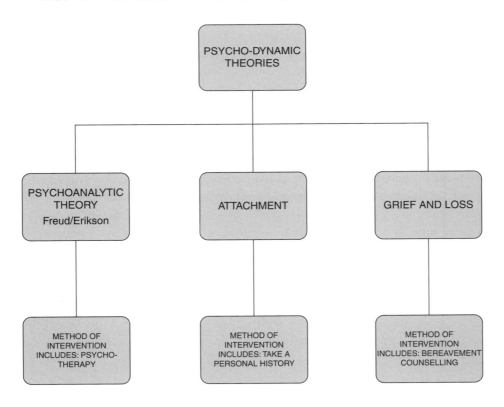

Freud's theory of psycho-sexual development

An introduction to psycho-dynamic theory has to begin with its founder, Sigmund Freud (1865–1939). This Austrian psychiatrist developed the 'treatment' for neuroses, namely psychoanalysis.

The main ideas

Many of our mental processes necessary for thinking occur subconsciously, beneath our consciousness, so we are not aware of them. This **unconscious mind** influences our thoughts, feelings and consequently behaviour in a way that by definition we cannot be fully aware of and do not have access to ourselves. There are three primary components of personality:

> » the **id**, which is concerned with satisfying instinctual drives and desires;

> » the **ego**, which is concerned with the compromise and control of the id in recognition of the social world and the consequences of unfettered id-driven behaviour;

> » the **superego**, which is concerned with the imposition of a morality on the way it seeks to mediate the conflicts between the id and ego.

In terms of child development, the baby and early toddler is solely id-driven but through socialisation by the caregivers the ego develops and with the child's ability to think conceptually the superego develops, manifest as conscience.

Our personality and its traits are the result of the interplay between the id, ego and superego; ideally, some balance is achieved. However, if one is dominant over the other then this too is reflected in the personality and its traits, often with associated behaviour. For example, someone whose need for instant gratification overrides the consideration of any consequences would be id-dominant. Dominance of the ego may manifest in a trait of being overly cautious or risk-averse whereas dominance of the superego may result in a trait of being overly controlling or authoritarian.

We are well fortified psychologically and seek to further protect ourselves from thoughts and feelings that cause anxiety by employing **defence mechanisms**. There are a number of defence mechanisms identified within this tradition. I will introduce a few of them, the first being *repression*.

Repression

We protect ourselves (our psyches) from hurt and pain and any trauma experienced by **repressing** such experiences and how they made us feel; but they do not disappear, they can dwell in the unconscious. However, such powerful thoughts and feelings demand expression and can find this by acting out in our behaviour. For example, repressed anger could express itself in the personality trait of having low impulse control.

Other defence mechanisms are:

Splitting is where contradictory thoughts and feelings are managed by compartmentalising them. For example, someone we love has treated us unkindly, which is resented. It is difficult to hold thoughts of love and resentment at the same time so we split these, expressing one or the other as if they were the total sum of our feelings towards the person.

Denial is where there is apparent refusal to acknowledge or accept the *reality* of a situation and it is either denied, or its impact minimised. For example, the caregiver of a child who is neglected seems to fail to acknowledge the consequences for the child.

Displacement is where a response to a situation is displaced from the original environment to another; for example, an employee who has been sacked may not protest the injustice suffered in the workplace but might do so at home, remonstrating with their partner as if they were the boss.

Projection is where hostile feelings are projected onto a person or concept to conceal an unacknowledged fear of being inclined to the behaviour or the concept being rejected. For example, a strong homophobic stance as opposed to a *live and let live* attitude may be the result of *projection*.

Within a therapeutic relationship there exists the potential for the 'client' to come to 'see' the therapist as representing the person in the relationship they are working on, a parent, for example. This phenomena is known as **transference**. Equally, the client may 'pull triggers' in the therapist which have the potential to distort the therapeutic relationship. This is known as **counter-transference**. In Patrick Casement's definition from *On Learning from the Patient* (2014), he states that the trigger for transference can begin in either the helper or the client. Where it begins is transference and how the other person responds to it is counter-transference. So, a helper might believe his or her role is to lead and direct the client and the counter-transference from the client is to 'become' helpless. Equally, the client can begin by being 'helpless' and the counter-transference response from the helper is to tell the client what to do.

The therapist or other professional involved in a therapeutic/helping relationship needs to be aware of these ideas and be sensitive to any thoughts or feelings the client invokes in them, as transference and counter-transference, if ignored, can result in the duty owed to the client by the therapist to provide the best service they can being undermined. In a therapeutic relationship the social worker should work towards *doing themselves out of a job* and avoid either creating dependency in their service user or allowing change on the part of their service user to depend on them. For example, I once worked on anger management behaviour with a teenager who was in care. As part of the work I met and interviewed his mum who had been a lone parent to the teenager. On leaving I became conscious of feeling quite angry myself and later concluded this was the result of having listened to a series of injustices that had befallen the mother. It was as if I was angry *on her behalf*. It was instructive as had my response been purely sympathetic, I would have supported her denial of any responsibility for these events. Furthermore I was conscious that if I could feel angry after an hour and a half, what might 15 years have done?

More controversial than the ideas introduced so far is Freud's family drama as played out though his **stage theory of psycho-sexual development**.

This begins with the **oral stage** (from birth to 18 months). This stage is characterised by the id and the source of satisfaction being feeding. The nipple or teat is the all-important world and this experience lays down a strong association with the id's **pleasure principle**. An illustration of this association is if the adult takes up smoking. There may be a variety of reasons why someone decides to smoke but it is an oral pleasure. A common substitute for the habit when the smoker tries to stop is eating sweets, another oral pleasure.

The next stage is the **anal stage** (from 18 to 36 months). The process of toilet training presents the child with the opportunity to begin to exert some control (over elimination), which can be pleasurable in itself and elicit approval from caregivers. However, if 'accidents' or perceived lack of progress is responded to critically by the caregiver a conflict is created in the child, which can result in a sense of confusion and possibly shame. The adult trait associated with this stage is a desire to exert control over the immediate environment.

The next stage is the **phallic stage** (3–5 years). Awareness of and interest in one's body, especially the genital area, is dominant in this stage and the child comes to harbour a sense of establishing a relationship above and beyond that of child to caregiver to that more akin to fantasising about becoming the partner of the parent of the opposite sex to them. Although this might, on the face of it, appear somewhat perverse, the idea is presented as a 'normal' characteristic of this stage and not born of dysfunction or the product of grooming or abuse. The conflict in this stage being the fact that the position of partner to the other caregiver is already taken, thus the child is cast as a rival. It is perhaps more accurate to think of this desire being closer to possession than a sexual or reciprocated relationship. The fear of their desire being discovered results in the **Oedipus complex** for boys seeking possession of their mothers and the **Electra complex** for girls seeking possession of their fathers.

We might speculate on the issue of power here as we have the id-driven sense of omnipotence conflicting with the developing restraint of the ego. However, the consequences for boys seem rather more threatening; their anxiety is the fear of being castrated by their father. Perhaps the best thing a father could say to his son in this stage would be to reassure him that he was not going to castrate him but it would seem a rather strange conversation (see the case of *Little Hans*). To the chagrin of feminists this stage witnesses a fundamental injustice to females. The stage is not solely characterised by an interest in one's body but also that of other children and comparison is inevitable. The girl is intrigued by what she doesn't have compared to boys, resulting in **penis envy**.

It should not be forgotten that during all this, the id, ego and latterly superego are developing and exercising their influence as the phallic stage gives way to the **latent stage** (5–12 years) in which there is less interest in matters sexual and sensual, the emphasis being on developing same-sex friendships with peers, abilities and skills.

The onset of puberty heralds the **genital stage** (12–20 years) in which the young person becomes sexually active, and develops into an independent adult.

A feature of these stages is the need to run the gauntlet of some particular conflict. The extent to which we 'resolve' the conflict and *come out the other end* of these stages, it is suggested, exerts a qualitative impression on our childhood and is influential on the development of personality, having the capacity to establish traits. Where a conflict is unresolved a corresponding trait results, giving the notion of a **fixation** to the stage concerned. This may not manifest in anything other than a tendency to behave in a particular way as opposed to another and is not usually associated with dysfunction that could disrupt or cause interference with the living of one's life. However, where a stage has not been sufficiently 'worked through', the need to undergo it will not have been satisfied, resulting in a desire to **regress**, behaviourally, to the age appropriate for the stage, irrespective of one's chronological age, creating an opportunity to undertake the stage again and resolve, more successfully, the conflict it presents. This 'treatment' is known as **regression therapy**.

Finally, there is the issue about what to do about all this given that much of it may be little more than the art of living. Equally, why should people have to go through their lives being in some way less happy or fulfilled than they would be were they not carrying around some residual issue from their childhood that hampers them? The standard therapy is, of course, psychoanalysis, in which the analyst identifies the repressed thoughts and feelings hidden in both the **free association**, in which the client is asked to just talk, and in the **dreams** of the person undergoing the therapy. The goal of the analyst is to bring these repressed thoughts and feelings into the 'acceptable' consciousness of the client. Psychoanalysis usually requires a long-term commitment to be *in therapy* and is costly. It is therefore unlikely to appeal to the many who engage in other forms of talking therapies on the continuum of psychotherapeutic interventions but not psychoanalysis. Such interventions might address specific issues, for example, bereavement counselling.

Some personal reflections on Freud's ideas

Clearly these ideas present some challenges. The extent to which they were substantiated empirically was weak and is likely to remain so; one is after all speculating on the subconscious and one could be 'in denial' if they were rejected. Accordingly, proving the substance of these ideas to anything like a scientific standard is likely to elude us. I think that the ideas make a significant contribution to the discourse on human motivation and merit consideration. They were born of a time and within a cultural context but undeniably a huge industry has grown from their origin.

Freud did not deny the incidence of sexual abuse; indeed, from his clinical practice he initially thought he was hearing accounts of such experiences. He famously 'changed his mind' about the origins of the symptoms and recollections of his 'patients', deciding they were more akin to fantasies and developed the ideas as described in the *family drama* of psycho-sexual development. There remains speculation about the reasoning behind Freud's change of mind. He included his own childhood experiences in his rationale and undertook the *talking therapy* himself. Viennese society of the day was appalled by the alleged incidence of incest and sexual abuse but Freud should have been able to anticipate such a reaction and I would be surprised if he capitulated to public opinion. Perhaps for now we have to accept the rather complex and confused picture of recovered and false memory syndrome we hear reported today.

An area that can cause unease is the emphasis Freud places on sex and sexual expression. In the stages prior to the genital stage children are not sufficiently sexually mature to engage in sexual expression as such but he held that sexual/sensual energy, **the libido**, is a very important drive associated with the id.

I asserted that there were some challenges within the ideas; I find it difficult to determine the extent to which they might 'hold sway' in comparison with other forces in society. For example, the people in post Second World War society in the UK were considered *healthy* in dietary terms as reflected in a BMI profile and is in stark contrast to the current incidence of obesity in the UK's population. Perhaps such changes might be explained by the imposition of rationing and the successful marketing of foods high in fat and sugar content. However, despite the abundance of such foods nowadays, not everyone is overweight or obese. Are we to conclude that those who find such foods difficult to resist are orally fixated? If so, how did the proportion of the post-war population who were orally fixated manage their unmet need? Surely such speculation is condemned to remain a matter of conjecture.

I will conclude these reflections by recounting an experience I had when working as a residential social worker. A teenager had been 'discovered' in the community but had not been a participant of it and had not been the recipient of universal services such as education and health. The young person's parents had, misguidedly, sought to 'protect' their child from society. The staff in the unit receiving the young person into care considered how best to manage and support the young person through this difficult transition. Of particular concern was that up until the young person's reception into care, a dummy was used for several hours per day, on occasion only being removed for the purpose of taking food or drink and at night. Freud proposed that some degree of fixation is likely to result where the conflict presented in a 'stage' is not resolved. The likelihood of the individual successfully resolving the conflict in a stage is optimised when the circumstances associated with the conflict cause the least anxiety. This includes the manner in which the stage is managed by the caregiver. The conflict in the oral stage is the transition weaning presents, which can involve the loss of pleasure and intimacy. Premature or overly delayed weaning due to overly rigid or relaxed attitudes to its management could add to the anxiety around this conflict, producing associated, subconscious 'hang ups' resulting in fixations.

This may seem an extreme example and one could not fail to be struck by the perverse outcome of the parenting practice the young person was subject to, the objective being 'protection' but resulting in increased vulnerability. The application of a Freudian-based analysis is not difficult to make. The young person concluded their weaning upon reception into care but the 'therapy' was not regression therapy or psychoanalysis. Medication was prescribed to help the young person counter the anxiety caused by the initial reduction in use and finally the total loss of the dummy, so great was the psychological dependency and consequential trauma the loss represented.

I have given the most rudimentary sketch of the main ideas of Freud and some who have developed his ideas, namely his daughter Anna in developing the ideas around defence mechanisms and Carl Jung and the Electra complex. Further reading dedicated to these complex ideas is required for the reader to be able to come to an informed decision as to the importance they should attract. However appreciative or otherwise you decide to be about Freud and his ideas, I think he can legitimately claim to have put the child's psyche on the map and in so doing established the qualitative import-ance of childhood.

Erikson's theory of psycho-social development

E Erikson (1902–1994) was a pupil of the school of Freudian psychotherapy. Erikson trained as a psychotherapist himself and devised his own stage theory of develop-ment, namely his **psycho-social theory of development.** Erikson is often referred to as a Neo-Freudian, *neo* meaning 'new or revived form of'. Many clinicians' and theorists' names are prefixed with this, which simply implies they have taken the basic ideas of whomever (Freud in this case), and built upon them with their own interpretation. In this case Erikson extended his stages into the life course. Perhaps the essential distinction Erikson's theory makes to that of Freud's is the recogni-tion of environmental influences, as indicated in the title, which infers that develop-ment is the product of the mind *and* society. A useful table setting out a comparison between Freud's and Erikson's stage theories of development can be found in Margarete Parrish's book *Social Work Perspectives on Human Behaviour* (Parrish, 2010, p 65). As with all stage theories, each stage presents a challenge, conflict or crisis the individual is confronted by and has to traverse. The quality with which the stage is traversed is influential on both the person and their approach to subsequent stages.

The theory begins with **trust v mistrust** (birth to 18 months), during which the infant is introduced to the extent to which they may be confident in having their needs responded to and met. If this can be relied upon they develop trust; if not, mis-trust is the outcome. (Note the congruence with attachment theory discussed later.) Next is **autonomy v shame, doubt** (18 months to 3 years), during which the toddler starts to explore and relate to the world around them, manage their will and develop self-control. If these early forages into the external world go well with acceptance and success, the child develops a sense of autonomy; if not, they develop a sense of embarrassment and shame. The next stage is **initiative v guilt** (3–5 years). This is to some extent a consolidation of the previous stage as the child becomes more sophisticated in their learning and exploration. An increasing sense of mastery and success through experimentation will produce the confidence to undertake greater initiatives whereas the opposite would produce more negative experiences. (See the discussion on the work of Bruce Perry.) Next is **industry v inferiority** (5–12 years). This stage is characterised by the further development of competence in abilities and skills, including the contribution made to group and team work. Envisage the powerful messages sent by failing the 11+ exam or being the last to be picked for the football or netball team.

The next stage is **identity v role confusion** (12–20 years). This stage oversees the often turbulent and angst-ridden adolescence, during which questions may be posed such as: Who am I? What do I stand for? The period often features risk-taking behaviours, experimentation and experiences in sexual orientation and intimate relationships. The goal in this stage is the establishment of an identity. The next stage is **intimacy v isolation** (approx. 20–25 years or young adulthood). The goal in this stage is concerned with the ability to form and sustain significant relationships based on emotional care and reciprocity. Middle adulthood is the next stage (approx. 25–65 years) and the crisis in this period is **generativity v stagnation**. This stage is concerned with the ability to balance competing needs and responsibilities. For example work ~ life, one's own needs ~ the needs of others, partner/family. Proactive engagement in life and continuing to find it meaningful is the challenge in this phase. The final stage is late adulthood (over 65) and the challenge in this stage is maintaining **integrity v despair**. Maintaining a sense of good mental health and emotional well-being is the objective in the life stage where there is increasingly less life left to live than what has gone before.

Some personal reflections on Erikson's ideas

As with Freud's theory, the extent to which Erikson's theory of psycho-social development remains relevant in offering an explanation of what troubles people and deprives them from optimising a sense of well-being will be tested by time. Already, the extent to which the ideas might be considered eternally universal to the human condition seems to be giving way to being an insightful but limited discourse, subject to its time and place. Furthermore, the way in which these ideas appear deterministic can be uncomfortable if one's belief in the potential for optimism and change is unbounded. The 'goals' set out in the theory present a useful set of objectives for each of the 'stages' encountered. However, it might be more helpful to think of the *outcome* as being on a continuum, the *ideal objective* being at one end and the *least favourable result* at the other, rather than a purely dualistic option of either intimacy *or* isolation being achieved.

In reviewing these ideas I am reminded of Dr Bruce Perry's work (2001). Bruce Perry is an American child psychiatrist who has specialised in treating children who have experienced trauma. He has stressed the importance of curiosity, describing it as the fuel of development. He suggests that curiosity is *hard-wired* into infants and should be encouraged by caregivers. The following table sets out the developmental benefits where curiosity is nurtured and allowed to flourish.

Curiosity	results in	Exploration
Exploration	results in	Discovery
Discovery	results in	Pleasure
Pleasure	results in	Repetition
Repetition	results in	Mastery
Mastery	results in	New Skills
New Skills	results in	Confidence
Confidence	results in	Self-esteem
Self-esteem	results in	Sense of Security
Sense of Security	results in	More Exploration

A toddler is playing outside the back door after it has rained; her attention is drawn to a bird digging for food in the moist soil next to the path. She goes to where it has been digging and puts her fingers in the earth, feeling its texture and smelling its rich odour. She finds a worm and watches it wriggle across her fingers. Her caregiver comes to see what she is up to. The caregiver draws her attention to a worm cast nearby and explains that's the worm's poo, after having eaten soil. The toddler squeals in delight at this and they go on to watch a snail crawl across the path carrying its spiral shell, leaving a slimy trail. The caregiver explains the shell is its home.

They go inside, the toddler washes her hands and at the suggestion of the caregiver draws a picture of the worm and the snail and tries to copy the stripy pattern in the snail's shell. The finished picture goes on the fridge door, and later the caregiver and toddler look into how the snail makes its home. Consider all the learning that would have been lost if the caregiver on seeing the toddler with her hands in the soil had simply chided her and said, *'That's dirty.'* Furthermore, consider the impact on the development of a child if the child lives in fear or where the caregiver discourages exploration, or the child lives in an understimulated environment. I find Dr Perry's work helpful and consider that it contributes to the development of a theme that I would like to argue has emerged from the ideas considered so far and is congruent with **attachment theory**, which, although within the psycho-dynamic tradition, is of significant importance to social work practice in any assessment of parenting capacity, individual placement decisions and policy regarding children's placements.

Attachment theory

Attachment theory is attributed to the work of John Bowlby (1907–1990) and was further developed by Mary Ainsworth (1913–1999) and associates. The main ideas in attachment theory are that human infants are universally 'hard wired' to seeking an attachment or bond with their primary caregiver and that ideally this is reciprocal. The complexity of how this attachment-seeking behaviour is manifest in the infant is in proportion to their cognitive development:

0–2 months. They are socially responsive but in a general sense. They respond to a human face, voice and interaction with them.

3–6 months. They continue to be socially responsive but this is now becoming differentiated. They recognise and demonstrate a preference for their primary caregivers.

7 months–3 years. The attachment behaviours of seeking proximity to and wanting the attention of the primary caregiver and their being preferred is clearly evident. The 'quality' of the attachment relationship is developing and becoming established.

3+ years. The attachment behaviours are becoming increasingly sophisticated and reciprocal between the child and their primary caregivers.

(Howe et al, 1999, p 20)

Establishing an attachment relationship is especially important during the *formative years* (birth to five years) and the way in which the attachment-seeking behaviour is responded to is influential in the development of personality, self-concept and consequently, future relationships. Bowlby observed infants who were separated from their primary caregiver (usually mothers, hence the term **maternal deprivation**) and found a sequential response of initially **protest**, after time, **despair** and again after time, **detachment** to be common in those children observed. He coined the term **separation anxiety** as the basis for the child's initial distress. Upon reunion the infants typically displayed anger, crying, clinging and rejection (Howe et al, 1999, p 12). Initially an emphasis was placed on the importance on the attachment to the child's mother and on maintaining the consistency of this if problems in adult life were to be avoided, but this has come to be considered as perhaps overly determin-istic. The emphasis is now placed on the importance of attentive primary caregiv-ers and not solely focussing on the role of the mother (Beckett and Horner, 2015, p 125), who are reliable in their responsiveness to attend to the child's needs appropri-ately. These needs span the range from the provision of food to affection. Picture the toddler who realises that they have explored beyond their safety zone and becomes distressed, turning to the direction of their caregiver and putting their arms out; in response, the caregiver attends to, picks up and reassures the child. In so doing, the message conveyed to the child is '*I can develop trust and confidence in having my needs responded to and met*'. The subtext of this message is that the world is a safe place. It is the consistency and reliability of this attentive, **attuned** response that builds a **secure attachment**.

Now consider that same scenario in which the child displays the same attachment-seeking behaviour of being distressed and needing attention and reassurance, but instead of responding with acceptance the primary caregiver expresses annoy-ance. Here the message conveyed to the child is that their neediness is a nuisance, undermining its authenticity. What do you think is the best course of action for the child's **adaptive response** to this caregiver? The child does not want to generate any more disapproval in the caregiver so they minimise their neediness. Where this response becomes sufficiently typical it can develop into an **avoidant attachment** style. The style is characterised by an avoidance of a close emotional bond; it is more tentative.

Consider the same scenario again. This time the child cannot elicit a response from the caregiver. It's as though the child and their needs failed to register and prompt a response from the caregiver. What do you think is the best course of action for the child's **adaptive response** to this caregiver? They will protest more in an effort to gain the attention of the caregiver and elicit a response from them. Where this response becomes sufficiently typical it can develop into an **ambivalent attach-ment** style. This style is characterised by indifference on the part of the caregiver to the needs of the child and an unsatisfied degree of neediness on the part of the child.

With avoidant and ambivalent attachments the child learns to apply an adaptive strategy in an attempt to elicit the *best* response they can achieve from the care-giver. They come to 'know' their caregiver and may delay presenting their need until circumstances are more favourable, in either mood or situation, to being addressed. Where responses are sufficiently consistent so as to become predictable the child can 'pick' the caregiver's behaviour which is why it is an *adaptive response* to the caregiver. For example, Amy has an avoidant attachment style with her mother. Her father is more accommodating of her but he defers decisions to his wife so as to not cause additional friction in an often fraught marital relationship. Amy's school is running an extra-curricular trip to the ballet in London and she would love to go. She needs her parents' agreement to meet the cost and would need to be picked up from the bus late in the evening. She doesn't want her parents to row about this so she decides to ask her mum but delays doing so as they have had an argument. She waits for things to calm down and chooses the optimal time likely to produce the outcome she wants, such as when her mum is in a good mood.

Finally, consider running the scenario through again. However, this time the caregiver is under the influence of substances, or is suffering an episode of a mental health issue; in any event the caregiver's emotional availability to respond to the child is compromised and not predictable. If this is case the child cannot easily develop an adaptive response as they cannot 'pick' the carer's behaviour. This results in **disorganised attachment**. Children subjected to abuse or traumatised in other ways such as by witnessing domestic abuse are likely to display symptomology associated with this attachment style such as withdrawal or *frozen watchfulness*. The 'message' communicated to children subjected to this style of attachment is the opposite to that of a secure attachment. Disorganised attachment creates an uncertain, fearful world in which the relationship between cause and effect cannot be trusted, denying the child autonomy and confidence in themselves and others.

These 'messages' are the subtext of what is communicated in the dominant attachment style the child experiences and become **mental representations** or an **internal working model** of which the child's self-concept is comprised and includes perceptions of self-worth, respect and esteem. When such concepts become qualitatively internalised they frame expectations of how they will be responded to by others. These expectations can be confirmatory and to some extent become self-fulfilling prophecies. I was reminded about this recently when leaving a yoga class. I noticed the laces of one of the participants' trainers had come undone and brought this to her attention in case she tripped. Her reply of '*I knew someone would remind me about that*' is indicative of someone with a secure attachment.

The dominant attachment style and the consequential 'messages' conveyed which help to build the internal working model influences personality development; accordingly, their **effect** can be extended into the life course.

The traits associated with secure attachment are those of balance, and being a well-rounded individual, whose emotions and that of others are authentic, who are autonomous and confident in their own ability to contribute and have that contribution accepted by others.

The traits associated with avoidant attachment include some degree of pseudo-maturity (one has after all minimised one's childhood needs) and of the individual not being at ease with emotions, preferring to *get on with it* in a matter-of-fact way, being self-reliant and playing down their own needs; and being reserved is preferred to closeness, which would be uncomfortable.

The traits associated with ambivalent attachment include: the need for attention, which could remain unsatisfied even if attended to. The neediness in childhood that was not responded to can leave a hunger for need to be met, overdependence on people, and the need for closeness and reassurance may both be present and mistrusted if provided.

The traits associated with disorganised attachment are numerous and include aggressive, controlling and coercive behaviours, higher than average incidence of depression and psychological disorders. This attachment style is characterised by fearfulness and conflict that is difficult to resolve and come to terms with. Those to whom the infant looks for attachment are also a source of fear and anxiety and can produce an overwhelmingly negative view of one's self-concept and the prospect that others are likely to value them, resulting in the worth of others being undermined.

Attachment styles, relationships and parenthood

David Howe et al's book, *Attachment Theory, Child Maltreatment and Family Support* (1999), provides a detailed account of attachment theory and its consequences. Unsurprisingly, given that essentially it is a theory about personality development it makes some predictions about the type of relationships people seek and have, and the type of parent one might become, based on the attachment style experienced during infanthood. Some of these predictions, paraphrased from Howe's book, are given below.

Those who experienced a secure attachment are best placed to, on occasion, 'park' their own needs and create the space necessary to attend to the needs of partners and children in an efficacious manner.

Those who experienced an avoidant attachment can engage in functional relationships with partners and children but emotional closeness would not be a strong feature of the relationship. Furthermore, giving authenticity to the emotions of others may be *played down* as it is not an area those with avoidant attachments are comfortable with.

Those who experienced an ambivalent attachment style again engage in functional relationships with partners and children but these relationships may be characterised by their residual neediness. The extent to which this is amenable to be satisfied in relations with partners and children will depend on their ability to resolve the conflict presented to the child during their infancy. Those who find this difficult are at risk of experiencing numerous relationships in the (likely to be frustrated) quest to find one in which their needs are met.

Those who experienced a disorganised attachment style will find establishing and maintaining functional, largely satisfactory relations with partners and children especially difficult to achieve due to the damaging nature of their childhood experiences. They are at risk of dysfunctional relationships and may demonstrate *acting out* behaviours of overt control and aggression linked to an inability to come to terms with those experiences and the loss involved in not having had significant needs met.

Some personal reflections on attachment theory

I find the claim of attachment theory being universally applicable to human beings to be credible and congruent with the behaviour exhibited by other primates who are biologically closely related to humans such as chimpanzees. Of the ideas discussed so far it is of particular significance to social work practice, notably in assessing parenting capacity and decision-making in children's placements. The reduction in the timeframe for care and adoption proceedings and the endeavours to reduce the number of placements experienced by looked after children are developments that have come about as a consequence of the understanding that infants and young children have a limited 'window of opportunity' to form an attachment to a primary carer(s).

Inherent in any theory of explanation is some degree of determinism, of cause and effect and consequently some implied limitation of the *effect* or outcome that can be achieved, unaided, owing to their *cause*.

Theories are often presented in a dualistic manner; one is either one thing or another, and they cannot reflect the complexity of reality and the nuances of social interaction and intimate relations. Consequently it is difficult, in a generalised way, to 'factor in' the individual characteristics of **adaptability, temperament,**

resilience and **vulnerability**, which is why accurate assessment and astute analysis is so important to social work intervention. These difficulties do not detract from the benefits the application of attachment theory can bring to understanding human behaviour. They do, however, require that application to be individually honed. For example, child A has an ambivalent attachment style with her primary caregiver. Despite this she has a sunny disposition which adults like, she has a friend, a nursery school assistant 'looks out' for her and a member of her extended family 'roots for her' and enjoys having her to stay on occasions. Such factors mitigate the effects of having an ambivalent relationship with a primary caregiver and if maintained and built upon will promote resilience in the child. Child B also has an ambivalent relationship with his primary caregiver but is sullen and isolated; if these characteristics remain unaltered they are likely to increase his vulnerability to the adverse effects of an ambivalent attachment style. It would be an early objective of a social worker, working with child B to:

» identify existing resilience factors and capitalise on them;

» identify potential opportunities for boosting factors of resilience;

» identify missing factors of resilience and explore ways to introduce and establish them or compensate for their absence.

The social worker should consider opportunities within the individual, their family and the wider community for building resilience across the following factors:

1. Opportunities for child B to experience features of a *secure* style towards him or her.

2. Education

3. Friendships

4. Talents and interests

5. Positive values

6. Social competencies

(Daniel, 2003, pp 13–14)

The role that **praise** can play in building resilience cannot be underestimated. I devised the following mnemonic as part of a training pack for early years workers:

Promote Resilience And Increase Self-Esteem

Although attachment theory emphasises the importance of the *formative years* and suggests that the quality of formative experience has lifelong consequences, the die cast is not absolutely fixed; the person is not inexorably condemned to the stated outcomes. We can learn from subsequent experiences throughout the life course and perhaps be fortunate enough to enjoy friendships and relationships that nullify and counter those negative messages acquired when young.

There is a powerful message coming from a summation of these psycho-dynamic based theories that can be represented through the following points:

Early childhood matters.

The quality of experiences and relationships in childhood resonates through the life course.

The extent to which our needs were met in infancy and early childhood constructs our self-concept and a platform from which we view our place in the world.

This is not, however, forever fixed and can be manipulated through therapy or mitigated though 'therapeutic' relationships.

There is one more stage theory, which although not chronologically developmental as such, lies within the psycho-dynamic school. I want to introduce this theory and encourage social workers to always consider its impact on the people they work with; it concerns their reaction to significant loss or bereavement. Important contributions have been made to the understanding of this phenomena, so common to the human condition, by Mia Kelmer Pringle et al (1986), Elizabeth Kubler-Ross (1969) and Colin Murray Parkes (1998), derived from their work with the dying and bereaved. They have slight differences in their 'stages' but the following sequence is generally representative of the reaction to loss and bereavement:

Initially there is **denial/disbelief**, moving to **preoccupation** with **yearning, seeking**, 'looking for', accompanied with flashes of **anger** when the frustrated desire for what is lost has to be confronted. It is as if the realisation of the loss can only be internalised in *bite-size* amounts. The next stage is characterised by **disorganisation, depression and despair** as acceptance (of the fact) begins. The final stage is **resolution**, an **emotional re-grouping** allowing calm and **coming to terms** with the loss. It is difficult to be specific about the timescale for this process, given individual differences and differences in the circumstances but one to two years would not be considered out of the ordinary.

Some personal reflections on the stage theory of loss or bereavement

Any stage theory is necessarily predictive of what (is likely) to happen. A more rigid interpretation might suggest it is predictive of what *should* happen and *by when*, which creates the opportunity for 'doing it wrong' and needs to be avoided. Perhaps the emphasis needs to be on a fluid interpretation, focusing on the well-being of the person, establishing if they have been able to come to terms with the loss or bereavement rather than being stuck somewhere earlier in the process and continuing to grieve the loss. I have deliberately used the terms loss *or* bereavement and would anticipate symptomology of the process in response to any significant loss as well as bereavement. This could include: the loss of a (living) unknown biological parent; the loss of birth parents or caregivers, siblings, friends, pets etc; when children are taken into care or experience placement moves; the loss of the 'original life' for an adopted child. These examples also involve the loss of a child or children to the *family of origin* where provision of substitute family care was necessary.

Application of psycho-dynamic theory to social work practice

The application of psycho-dynamic theory is significantly restricted within mainstream social work practice owing to the fact that unless the social worker is also a trained psychotherapist, they cannot attempt to 'treat' their service user in the customary methods associated with this school. Furthermore, the appropriateness of a programme of psychoanalysis would be questionable given that most social work intervention with children and families is undertaken to safeguard and promote the welfare of children, through *early help offers* (see Chapter 1 of *Working Together to Safeguard Children*, 2015) or through *'children in need'* or in need of safeguarding (section 17 and 47 of the Children Act 1989). Under such intervention the child is the primary service user and an improvement in their circumstances through addressing the concerns that triggered the referral and found in any subsequent assessment is required in shorter timescales than is usually associated with being *in therapy*. Nevertheless, the erudite social worker should be mindful of the ideas within the psycho-dynamic school for a variety of reasons, including the recognition of transference and to guard against the risk of counter-transference, recognition of the possibility of being in denial, repression or being 'stuck' in a stage as well as the ideas relating to attachment which are essential in assessing parenting capacity.

Case study

Annette is a white 23-year-old woman with two children: a baby, Sam, aged 18 months and a toddler, Ben, aged two and a half. They live in a small rural town. Her current partner, Andy, is an intravenous drug user who lives part of the time at Annette's; the rest of the time he spends at friends who live in a bigger town some 30 miles away. Sam and Ben are considered 'children in need' as defined in the 1989 Children Act and the social worker has begun a number of visits to update an assessment of how the children's needs are being met and to monitor the children's welfare and their home environment, both of which have been neglected at times. The social worker knows from the case files that Annette had a disrupted childhood, her name having been put on the child protection register for neglect, and she experienced frequent moves. She is estranged from her mother, her father died when she was 11 and she has little contact with extended family.

Regarding her childcare practices, the house shows signs of neglect and there are issues around hygiene: the social worker noticed a pile of dirty nappies heaped up in a corner of the living room. Annette's apparent 'open door' policy results in a number of people coming and going and on a previous visit the social worker noticed a number of people congregated in the home, two of whom she knew should have been at school. The supervision and some personal care of the children such as feeding and nappy changing appears to be quite disorganised and undertaken by a number of people.

How far does psycho-dynamic theory explain the presenting issues in the case study?

Unless the social worker is also a trained psychotherapist, a Freudian analysis of the behaviour described in the case study is not accessible as untrained speculation about this should be avoided. However, the proficient social worker could build an impression of Annette's internal working model and consequently her self-esteem and confidence in her own competence. Based on her personal history, the social worker could legitimately speculate on the attachment style Annette had with her carers. The extent to which she accurately reflected on her circumstances and took responsibility for them could indicate the extent of any denial or repression. Andy's drug use may also be the result of repression. The frequent moves, the extent to which her needs were adequately met, the death of her father, estrangement with her mother and little contact with extended family could represent significant losses. If any of these had not been grieved for or were still being grieved, this could be a drain on what emotional energy she has.

One final thought. Irrespective of your view on what psycho-dynamic theory has to offer a social worker, let's just say there is substance to it and missed or significantly unresolved 'stages' *do* need addressing through therapeutic intervention in order to move on healthily. It's a sobering thought that if this were true, no other intervention discussed in this book would produce significant and enduring change.

Intervention drawing on ideas from psycho-dynamic theory

The social worker would need to discover what **insights** Annette has about her past and would need to create the opportunity for some time to talk to Annette on a one-to-one basis, the objective being to take a **personal history** of Annette's recollections of her own childhood, events that she regards as significant, the nature of relationships to parents, carers, siblings, and people she considered important. This could indicate the attachment style she had with her caregivers and identify the **losses** she considers significant, perhaps offering an insight into the extent to which she has come to terms with these. Her childhood experience of social work intervention could be vitally important to her engagement and the outcome of the current intervention, and merits enquiry. Even if this was negative, the opportunity to **reframe** the potential for the current intervention should not be missed. For example, if in response to the social worker's question Annette replies, '*Well, the social worker was friendly enough and seemed interested in the beginning but nothing really changed for me*', the social worker could reply, '*I'm sorry to hear that we did not manage to improve things for you, but what about Sam and Ben, what do you want for them?*' Annette replies, '*Oh, I want things to be better for them*' and the social worker responds, '*Yes, that's really good to hear. OK, so how are we going to make things better for them?*' The social worker has begun to create a platform for intervention.

The social worker should be interested in Annette's assessment of where she is now and if this is where she wants to be; if not, what does she want to be different and what coping strategies does she use?

The social worker would also be interested in the importance of her relationship with Andy and the level of support she feels she receives from him and is she OK with this? The response to these two questions may give an insight into Annette's **internal working model** in terms of her expectations and what she considers she deserves.

If Annette considers Andy's role to be increasingly significant in relation to her and the children, he would need to be included in the assessment and any intervention. The social worker would be interested in his drug use, if Annette uses, its safe management and reasons for its use. The 'highs' obtained can serve to help **repress** difficult and painful thoughts and feelings and the social worker may wish to explore this.

Does the social worker feel they are receiving genuine responses from Annette? If Annette was well psychologically **defended**, by being in **denial** this could represent a block from seeing her current situation and the extent to which she was meeting the needs of her children clearly.

The social worker would want to know what the 'open door' was about in terms of its function. Does it provide support, help, friends, company? Or does she not seem able to 'police' her doorway? The answer to this is important as the social worker will be looking for this practice to reduce. She would want to see an increase in the extent to which Annette undertakes the care and supervision of Sam and Ben. Furthermore, it is not appropriate to encourage truancy but if this reduction represented a significant loss for Annette, without an appropriate substitute that met, at least in part, these otherwise lost needs, change would be unlikely to occur.

The social worker would also be interested in how Annette has come through the significant losses she considers herself to have experienced, including the death of her father. This may offer an insight into whether or not Annette has 'grieved' these to **resolution** or is still grieving these. The observation of the interaction between Annette and Sam and Ben would be essential in coming to an understanding of the development of their **attachment** to her and the 'style' that may be developing.

Some personal reflections on intervention, drawing on ideas from psycho-dynamic theory

The focus of much of the work undertaken by child and family social workers, especially where young children are concerned, is on the parent(s) or caregivers, as it is their parenting that needs to change if, as in this case, the children are likely to have the opportunity to achieve a reasonable standard of health and development within their childhood. Currently they do not enjoy this and hence fulfil the criteria as '*children in need*' (section 17 (10), Children Act 1989). The social worker needs to bear in mind the objective of their intervention, of improving the lot of the child. The caregivers are of course fundamental to this and spending time exploring their 'issues', conveying interest and respect with a goal of enhancing their ability as caregivers, will benefit the whole family. Some service users who have ambivalent attachment styles may present as very needy themselves and the social worker should avoid becoming their proxy counsellor or parent. I have seen numerous situations in which it appeared the resolution to the muddle of feelings resulting from unmet need in childhood was to become a parent. It was as if something that would be 'theirs' would offer love and acceptance unconditionally. The profound sadness of this dynamic is that it is the baby who needs parenting by caregivers able to prioritise the child's needs over those of their own.

Intervention drawing on ideas from psycho-dynamic theory is limited in application. However, it can offer important insights to inform the assessment and analysis the social worker needs to undertake. There is also an educative role for the social worker in helping the caregiver to enhance their parenting skills, their understanding underpinning such skills, and the importance of establishing as secure an attachment as possible with the child. It is unlikely to lead to therapeutic intervention in the strict sense unless access to such a service is signposted.

References and further reading

Beckett, C and Horner, N (2015) *Essential Theory for Social Work Practice*. London: Sage.

Casement, P (2014) *On Learning from the Patient* (2nd ed). Abingdon: Routledge.

Children Act 1989 (c.41). London: TSO. [online] Available at: www.legislation.gov.uk/ukpga/1989/41/contents (accessed 20 February 2017).

Daniel, B (2003) The Value of Resilience as a Concept for Practice in Residential Settings. *Scottish Journal of Residential Child Care*, 2(1): 6–15. [online] Available at: www.researchgate.net/profile/Brigid_Daniel/publication/264878107_The_Value_of_Resilience_as_a_Concept_for_Practice_in_Residential_Settings/links/55e95bb008aeb65162647b72.pdf (accessed 20 February 2017).

Department for Education (2015) *Working Together to Safeguard Children*. Manchester: Department for Education. [online] Available at: www.gov.uk/government/uploads/system/uploads/attachment_data/file/419595/Working_Together_to_Safeguard_Children.pdf (accessed 20 February 2017).

Howe, D, Brandon, M, Hinings, D and Schofield, G (1999) *Attachment Theory, Child Maltreatment and Family Support*. Palgrave: Basingstoke. [This textbook offers a detailed account of attachment theory.]

Kubler-Ross, E (1969) *On Death and Dying*. London: Routledge.

Murray Parkes, C (1998) *Coping with Loss*. Oxford: John Wiley.

Parrish, M (2010) *Social Work Perspectives on Human Behaviour*. Maidenhead: Open University Press.

Parrish, M (2014) *Social Work Perspectives on Human Behaviour* (2nd ed). Maidenhead: Open University Press. [See part 2, pp 47–92 for an overview of psycho-dynamic theory.]

Perry, B (2001) Curiosity: The Fuel of Development. *Early Childhood Development Today*, 15(6): 22–4.

Pringle, M L Kellmer, Great Britain Department of Health and Social Security, National Childrens Bureau (1986) *The Needs of Children: A Personal Perspective*, 3rd ed. London: Hutchinson.

Skynner, R and Cleese, J (1984) *Families and How to Survive Them*. London: Mandarin. [Psychotherapist Robin Skynner takes the inquisitive but essentially lay person John Cleese through some of the ideas in the psycho-dynamic tradition. Very readable.]

Sylva, K and Lunt, I (1989) *Child Development: A First Course*. Oxford: Blackwell. [Part 1 of this introductory reader addresses the psychology of development in an approachable manner. It includes the 'treatment' Freud recommended for *Little Hans*.]

BEHAVIOURAL THEORY

Headlines

Concerned with behaviour that can be observed and measured.

Human behaviour is a product of association and can be changed.

Behaviour is acquired by being learnt by observation, copying or specific training. What has not been learnt can be.

What has been learnt can be unlearnt and different behaviour can be learnt by observation, copying or specific training.

Our thoughts and feelings influence our behaviour. Changing our thoughts and feelings changes our behaviour

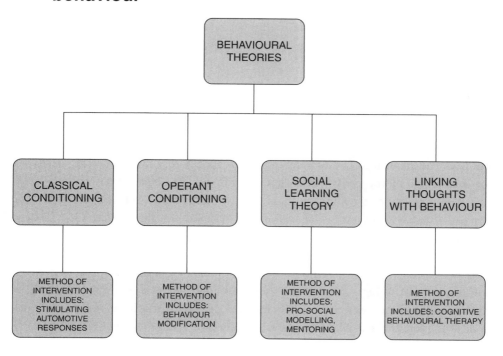

Classical or respondent conditioning

J B Watson (1878–1958) is considered the founder of the scientific study of behaviour known as behaviourism, developing the earlier work of Ivan Pavlov (1849–1936). The training Ivan Pavlov undertook with dogs is the textbook example of **classical or respondent conditioning**. Dogs naturally salivate at feeding times. Pavlov noted that they began to do this not solely when presented with food but did so in response to the associated behaviour of the feeder, such as getting the bowls and scooping the food into them. He famously experimented with ringing a bell simultaneously with feeding and after a little while the dogs would salivate in response to hearing the bell alone. This response would eventually disappear unless the ringing of the bell was re-associated with the presentation of food.

The emphasis in this form of **behaviour modification** is stimulating an **automotive response**. Like the dogs, we have little direct or conscious control of our automotive system. We breathe and our heart beats 'automatically'. If we are scared our bodies increase the adrenaline supply, preparing our muscles for *fight or flight*. A quickening heart rate and other effects such as hypervigilance and sweaty palms are further examples of automotive responses. Powerful experiences of the type that can trigger a fight or flight response can initiate what later becomes a phobia. There are few circumstances in which an intervention that is designed to trigger a response from the automotive system would be appropriate or ethical. One example is the use of medication such as Antabuse and Campral with those being treated for alcohol dependency, which results in biliousness if an alcoholic drink is imbibed.

Operant or instrumental conditioning

E L Thorndyke (1874–1949) and B F Skinner (1904–1990) are particularly associated with this other form of behaviour modification known as **operant or instrumental conditioning**. The fundamental idea here is that our behaviour is *shaped* or *conditioned* by the **consequences** it holds for us. Therefore, if we 'operate' (as if working a machine) the consequences, we will modify the (antecedent) behaviour. Particular behaviour is more likely to be exhibited and repeated if it produces desired outcomes or its consequences are valued; this is known as the **law of effect**. It is therefore amenable to modification if whatever acts as a reward for wanted behaviour or a disincentive for unwanted behaviour can be manipulated; this process is called **reinforcement**. Where a behaviour is conditioned out of being manifest, **extinction** is said to have been achieved. Behaviour can be positively reinforced in which a desired stimulus is used to maintain and increase wanted behaviour, for example, giving praise or material gain. It can also be negatively reinforced where an undesired stimulus is used to prompt a behaviour, for example, an annoying 'pinging' may sound in a car until the seatbelt is engaged. Within behaviourist literature, a distinction is made between negative reinforcement and punishments. Punishments are imposed to deter certain behaviour but are limited to that rather than to have a reinforcing effect that promotes the repetition of the desired behaviour.

Using operant conditioning to modify behaviour

It is possible to unwittingly reinforce unwanted behaviour. An exacting analysis and, on occasion, counter-intuitive response is required if this is to be avoided. Consider the child who, as we know from attachment theory, craves the attention of a primary caregiver. The caregiver does not give their attention to the child when the child is being good because the caregiver mistakenly regards good behaviour as being normal and not worthy of attention or praise. The message to the child is to get attention you have to *act up*. Where the child's need for the caregiver's attention is greater than the 'fear' of being told off, the child will act up. What should this caregiver do in response? If they give the child the attention in response to their acting up, they will reinforce the child's attention demanding through acting up behaviour. The caregiver *should* ignore the acting up behaviour. This is a brave strategy as what do you think the child's response would be to their acting up behaviour being ignored, especially if it had been reinforced previously by the caregiver? The child's acting up behaviour will worsen, increasing in its drama and distress, even to the point of a full-blown tantrum, which although difficult should continue to be ignored.

But this is only half of the caregiver's appropriate response using operant conditioning as so far reinforcing the unwanted behaviour has been avoided. After and separate from the incidences of the child's attention-seeking behaviour, the caregiver should choose a time when the child is exhibiting desired behaviour and then deliberately give attention, praise, express interest, whatever is appropriate to the situation, provided it serves to reinforce the desired behaviour. If the child had previously experienced their attention-demanding behaviour being reinforced by their caregiver, the process of behaviour modification as described could need to be repeated many times. It could be further reinforced with a daily (for severe cases) or a weekly *star chart* in which a reward would be 'earned' based on less than x number of tantrums per day or week, decreasing and moving to monthly, towards extinction.

There are some important considerations in devising a programme of behaviour modification. It must be applied with unswerving consistency. If multiple caregivers are involved, they need to ensure they respond consistently to the child's behaviour in accordance with the specific programme to discourage the unwanted behaviour and reinforce the desired behaviour. Careful consideration needs to be given to what is used as a reward. It has to be something that holds real value for the person being rewarded and ideally has integrity with rather than undermining the modified behaviour being maintained and habituated into skills for life and lifestyles.

For example, a socially isolated child who has undergone a programme of behaviour modification to improve their interpersonal skills could be rewarded with a new game for their Xbox. While perhaps the game is a desired reward, it would not create an opportunity for the child to practise their new behaviours as something more socially orientated would. A dieting group celebrating their success could reward themselves by going out for a slap-up meal or a day at a health spa.

Punishment and promoting consequentialism

The recidivism rates for ex-offenders and the often 'usual suspects' lined up outside the headteacher's office suggests that punishment alone is ineffective in modifying behaviour over intermediate and long-term timescales. The success of punishment in deterring certain behaviour is dependent on: an appreciation of the consequences the behaviour is likely to bring; and the desire to avoid those consequences being greater than the desire to exercise the behaviour that would incite them.

So far so good but there is a lot that can go wrong with making a rational connection between these two. The first part has to be achieved to even have options in respect of the second.

Consider the motorist who regularly drinks a couple of pints of mid-strength beer in his local pub and drives home. He knows he is close to exceeding the permitted alcohol/blood level but somewhat illogically is prepared to 'take the risk' in the belief that he is a safe driver after two or three pints, is unlikely to be stopped and breathalysed or would be 'just OK' if he was. The fear of the possibility of the punishment is less than the gratification anticipated and/or experienced by visiting the local pub and drinking the beer. Furthermore, the pleasure gained by visiting the local pub and drinking the beer is immediate, whereas the risk entailed can be pushed away. The 'immediacy' of this is of course reversed when he is stopped and asked to '*blow into the bag*'!

Being wise before the event is harder than being wise after it. The decisions we make as human beings have the potential to have integrity but undoubtedly some are un- or ill-considered; some involve risk-taking behaviour; some are based on a distorted concept of one's own infallibility; some are simply mistakes involving a combination of factors. In his book, *A Brief Introduction to Social Work Theory*, David Howe discusses a standard adaptation of behaviour modification to help make the link between cause and effect called the ABC of behaviour modification (Howe, 2009, p 56).

The objective of the ABC technique is to make the connection between behaviour and its consequences and in so doing create *options* rather than maintain a default outcome.

The technique requires a detailed analysis, almost frame by frame, of an example of the behaviour to be modified. It could be an act of violence such as an assault, a criminal offence, anything that merits enhancing the clarity of thinking around decision-making pathways.

The A stands for antecedents and an accurate analysis of these is essential to identify the sequence of escalation and the *triggers* for the perpetrator that lead to B, the behaviour. The C is for the consequences that resulted from the behavioural option chosen. The sequence is re-run, the environment remains the same as does the initial *perceived provocation* but this time the perpetrator is invited to think about their reaction(s) and consider if there were opportunities during the escalation phase and at the trigger points where their reaction could have been different, resulting in different behaviour and consequences. This would include recognising opportunities to de-escalate and not to have 'buttons pressed' or 'triggers pulled'. The *alternative scenario* should be rehearsed and could be role played, allowing the perpetrator to become better acquainted with and 'try out' the behavioural options the technique makes available to them. The technique of option creation could be run in conjunction with operant conditioning, reinforcing the wanted behaviour. For example, Jimmy had another period of exclusion from school following a fight with a pupil who had received minor injuries as a result:

Antecedent (provocation) = behavioural response (fight) = consequence (exclusion)

This was not the first of such incidents and Jimmy is acquiring a reputation of having a 'short fuse', getting into arguments and trouble. An analysis of the antecedents revealed a practical joke had been played on Jimmy which had 'wound him up'; a verbal altercation had ensued in which he was taunted about his ginger hair and he'd 'lost it' and lashed out, giving the other boy a bloody nose and bruising to his face. The ABC technique would focus on the first point of escalation, Jimmy's response to the practical joke, and invite him to consider alternative responses to being wound up, which may of course have provided the 'entertainment value' his peers may have sought.

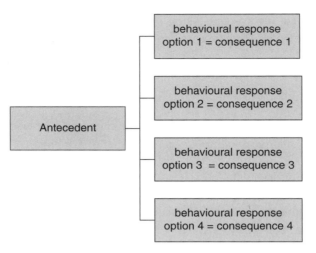

Figure 2.1 The ABC analysis of behaviour (theory)

A different reaction to the joke may have deescalated the scenario to the extent that the verbal altercation did not occur. Jimmy's reaction to the taunt could also be considered with a view to creating alternative reactions to that of *lashing out*.

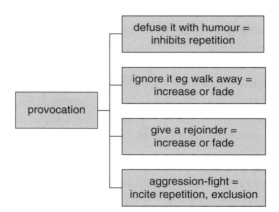

Figure 2.2 The ABC analysis of behaviour (applied)

Operant conditioning could be used to reinforce the work with the ABC technique by rewarding an increase in the number of occasions Jimmy had chosen alternative options in situations that hitherto would have prompted aggressive behaviour.

Another behavioural technique that promotes the recognition of the connection between an action and its consequence is to invite the person being worked with to analyse the costs or forfeits their current behaviour is likely to result in. For example, the worker draws the following table on a piece of flip chart paper, but then gives the marker pen to Jimmy who is asked to describe what happened (the behaviour) and its outcomes

Behaviour	Outcomes
The other kids at school wound me up, they tied my football boot laces together and I couldn't undo them, I swore at them, they took the **** calling me names, I got angry, lost it and hit one of them.	I got into trouble and was excluded from school for two weeks. The kid I hit got a bloody nose and bruising. His parents came to school and threatened to get me done by the police for assault unless I apologised.

Although Jimmy may feel his behaviour was justified, the worker draws attention to the fact that he is risking permanent exclusion, involvement of the police, and acquiring a criminal record unless his reaction to provocation changes. Some specific work might need to be done about how to 'save face' in de-escalation but the worker now concentrates on where Jimmy wants to be in one or two or five years. He is 14 years old now; the worker asks him to write down what he wants for himself in the next two to four years. Through discussion with the worker Jimmy identifies his aspirations and the worker draws his attention to the behaviours needed to support them.

Outcomes Jimmy wants in the next two to four years	Behaviour required to achieve these
I want to work as an agricultural mechanic like my uncle. I want some money in my pocket. I want to live independently, I want a girlfriend.	I need to complete my secondary education with the necessary GCSEs to attend agricultural college. I need to stay out of trouble and show I am reliable so I would stand a better chance of getting an apprenticeship, a job which would lead to having some money in my pocket and being able to take a girlfriend out.

The worker compares the diagrams on the two pieces of flip chart paper, inviting choices to be made towards the steps necessary to achieve his ambitions or more problems.

At the time of writing I am mindful of a case in Aberdeen, where on 9 March 2016, Bailey Gwynne, a 16-year-old boy, was stabbed and killed by a fellow pupil, also 16, over what started as an argument over a biscuit that lead to a taunt about being overweight. It is tragic that two young lives were ruined, one irrevocably, over something so comparatively trivial. Perhaps the ABC technique should be taught to all secondary school pupils as part of their PSHE education curriculum.

Social learning theory

Albert Bandura (1925–present) is particularly associated with this behaviourist theory which emphasises the reciprocal nature of the relationship between individual factors (self-concept and perceptions), the environment and one's behaviour. Bandura termed the interplay between this triad as **reciprocal determinism**. A celebrated experiment he undertook using Bobo dolls involved some children watching adults behaving aggressively with the dolls and a control group that did not. The former group went on to behave aggressively with the dolls, some modelling their behaviour on what they saw in the adults' behaviour; the control group did not behave aggressively with the dolls. This experiment revealed the importance of **observation** and **replication** in the acquisition of behaviour and the influence of the social context in which it is learnt. So this theory holds that we learn the behaviour we are exposed to, that which is 'modelled' for us.

The range and quality of our behavioural repertoire will be governed by the range and quality of the behaviour we have been exposed to. If the range experienced has been small then greater pressure is placed on the quality of what we have experienced in order to be 'tooled up' for the roles and responsibilities we are likely to encounter. If the range has been small and the quality poor, our behavioural repertoire will be limited, resulting in being ill-equipped to undertake these roles and responsibilities. However, with behaviourism, what has been learnt can be unlearnt and different behaviour can be learnt by observation, copying or specific training. So parents who don't know how to parent successfully can undergo parenting classes. A young person who has learnt anti-social responses to interpersonal communication can undertake a programme of **pro-social modelling**; a **mentor** could undertake this who would act as a role model. The selection of a mentor is important as it needs to be someone the person to be worked with would aspire to and would want to emulate.

For example, let's return to Jimmy. An assessment has revealed some of the cultural influences he has been exposed to, which include traditional 'masculine' role modelling where you don't sort things out by talking and it's better to 'get one in first'. This has taught Jimmy that the world is a hostile place, resulting in a 'readiness' towards adopting a defensive/aggressive stance. The discrimination he experiences by being ginger-haired supports this world view. Jimmy loves football and shows some talent; however, he has not been picked for the school team as he has acquired a reputation for being argumentative and a trouble-maker and is becoming increasingly marginalised in school.

Fortunately for Jimmy, a teacher at his school responsible for pastoral care is aware of these developments and under an 'early help offer' (see Chapter 1 of *Working Together to Safeguard Children*, 2015) has proposed Jimmy receives some additional support through a mentoring scheme. Jimmy's mentor is Matt, a post-16 pupil studying for A levels. He is popular with his peers, a keen sports player. He is also ginger-haired. He and Jimmy have devised a programme of activities to undertake together which includes attending a local football derby. The programme of mentoring provides an enjoyable, indirect way for Jimmy to be exposed to a pro-social model through Matt's social competence and positive outlook.

Linking thoughts with behaviour

The main theoretical framework within behaviourism that seeks to manipulate the association between what we think and our behaviour is **cognitive behavioural therapy**, known as CBT for short. It is not the only method of intervention that links cognition with behaviour. A programme of behaviour modification using the ABC analysis might well link thoughts and expectations around the escalation phase to challenge a behavioural default position in favour of expanding the behavioural options. However, analysing how we think and consequently feel about things, challenging this and changing it incrementally is central to a CBT intervention. CBT can work well with those who have sufficient cognitive development or ability to engage in this analysis.

Its early development as a therapy is associated with the American psychiatrist A T Beck (1921–present) and was primarily used to treat psycho-social conditions such as depression and anxiety disorders. Its use has developed to incorporate a wider range of applications.

The basic premise is that whenever people respond to a situation, how they *think* about it will shape their *emotional* response, which will give rise to any *physiological* changes required which will determine their *behavioural* response.

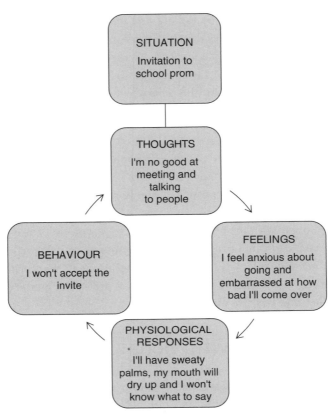

Figure 2.3 Behavioural analysis using CBT
Williams and Garland (2002)

These interdependent factors work together and produce appropriate reactions to situations where the starting point is a realistic and rational representation. They can, however, result in inappropriate responses to a situation if the starting point contains thoughts lacking in balance or are distorted. This of course describes irrational fears (phobias) as well as some compulsive behaviours and responses that could be considered dysfunctional, overly or under demonstrative or extreme.

If we think about applying CBT with Jimmy, the *situation* is the practical joke which leads to a verbal taunt and results in a fight. The therapist would want to know Jimmy's thoughts about peer relationships, those he thinks are good and not so good, the number of good and not so good relationships, the benefits of good relationships, what the prospect of contact with peers means to him, how he handles jokes and taunts etc.

It is important that the therapist hears and understands his specific answers but for the sake of this exercise and brevity the themes emerging from Jimmy's answers reveals he views relationships and contact as predominately combative and conflictual. He cites no 'good' relationships and struggles to identify any benefits from such relations. The prospect of contact means antagonism for Jimmy and his response to jokes and taunts is that they are going to be at his expense and make him angry.

The therapist will gently challenge these thoughts by testing them against reality. How many interactions with people over the last week resulted in conflict or a fight, the therapist might pose, the answer Jimmy would have to admit would be a minority, perhaps one or two out of dozens. This then discredits his claim to have no 'good' relations; they might not be 'pally' but most are not bad. He may have some 'homework' to do, identifying a situation in the forthcoming week which had 'wound him up' and to scale out of 1 to10 how angry he felt. This exercise would be repeated, the degree of anger decreasing as his thoughts yield to the more balanced 'world view' the therapist is exposing. There is also an educative role for the therapist in explaining how thoughts lead to feelings, feelings lead to behaviour, in so doing, increasing ownership and responsibility for behaviour by understanding its mechanism. CBT as with other behaviourist interventions are short term. The therapist might see Jimmy over six to ten sessions during which the therapist would 'hold a mirror' for Jimmy to see a more accurate view of reality, to re-set the register as to the true extent of 'conflict' in his life.

Similar ideas are employed when CBT is used to address phobias and other anxiety-related conditions but the physiological changes the feelings prompt are usually fight or flight responses and the sufferer experiences a genuine sense of fear and associated physiological symptoms at the prospect of being exposed to their phobia. So, in addition to challenging the actual 'threat' the phobia poses to the sufferer's existence, the therapist may also introduce a programme of **desensitisation** to the phenomena concerned. For example, Jimmy's presenting behaviour was not worked with earlier and a number of temporary exclusions contributed to his choosing avoidance as a way round his problem; he is refusing to attend school and is showing some symptoms of school phobia. A programme of desensitisation may include supporting Jimmy to manage the anxiety provoked when looking at a photo of his school, moving to being in the vicinity of the school to walking past his school, to visiting his school at a weekend, to actually attending initially perhaps half a day a week, building to three or four days towards full-time attendance.

There is one other idea I want to discuss but it comes with a caution about its application as it represents a strong, critical challenge and can produce a highly defensive reaction. It involves drawing attention to a lack of 'fit' between the thought and the behaviour. Where this lack of fit occurs **cognitive dissonance** is created. I was first introduced to this idea by a senior probation officer who had interviewed a convicted criminal for a report. The criminal had killed a number of women but in the interview he corrected the probation officer's description, supplanting the word *women* with *prostitute*. The probation officer demurred and the exchange was repeated three times by which point the criminal's white-knuckled clenched fists prompted the probation officer to conclude the interview. In the criminal's distorted thinking he could justify his behaviour as ridding the world of the prostitutes he'd killed but not if he thought of them as women.

I have used the technique in a few child protection cases, an example of which concerned a young girl whose body and head lice infection was described by the paediatrician who examined her as the worst she had ever seen. The child's father angrily protested against the involuntary intervention by social care, proclaiming that he loved the child very much. I did not dispute this directly but I asked him to conjure up in his mind a picture of a loved child. I then asked him how close the picture resembled his own child as presented to the hospital that day. Simulating such cognitive dissonance is a high-risk strategy, as it can prompt defensiveness and hostility, but I considered it worthwhile in this case to 'bring home' the seriousness of her maltreatment. After some time, during which a considerable amount of work was undertaken, the girl was returned to her parents' care.

Other ideas that can contribute to *self-fulfilling prophecies*

Martin Seligman coined the term **learned helplessness** (Parrish, 2014, p 117) to describe the phenomenon in which the service user appears to regard their situation; the 'quality' of the partners they attract; the way things will work out for them in the future etc, as being somehow inevitable. This essentially *passive* stance denies personal responsibility, dissociates cause and effect, and dismisses the possibility of being an active agent in the process of change. It serves to justify the status quo comfortably as there is little point in seeking change as such endeavours will fail. Seligman's concept of learned helplessness is limited in that he did not offer a specific therapy to address it. Perhaps challenging it through an existential approach may be appropriate (see Chapter 3).

Becker and Lemert coined the term **labelling** to describe how the social expectations of others can contribute to '*self-fulfilling prophecies*' (Payne, 2005, p 170).

An example of how this might work is if Jimmy had older brothers who had preceded him in school. In applying social learning theory, they are likely to have been exposed to similar role models and ideas and consequently may have behaved in a manner that established something of a 'reputation'. Jimmy enrols and it is not long before pupils and staff connect the surname and it is possible that in a variety of ways – some direct, some insidious – similar behaviour is anticipated, expected and even encouraged. This is of course a form of stereotyping and discrimination; perhaps the best way to address it is to ensure it is not a feature of our own practice.

Application of behaviourist theory to social work practice

Applying behaviourist theory to social work practice predominantly deals with the 'present', addressing *presenting behaviours*. CBT is often undertaken by clinicians within mental health services but not exclusively so. Interventions using behaviourist methods are usually short term and most of the techniques available under this theoretical framework lie within the range of skills a proficient social worker could be expected to have. The skills to apply CBT could be acquired through developing a practice specialism.

Behaviour modification using operant conditioning has a wide range of application. Unlike CBT it does not always require the utilisation of cognitive skills and so can be used with those whose cognitive ability is under developed through immaturity or impairment.

Case study

Annette is a white 23-year-old woman with two children: a baby, Sam, aged 18 months, and a toddler, Ben, aged two and a half. They live in a small rural town. Her current partner, Andy, is an intravenous drug user who lives part of the time at Annette's; the rest of the time he spends at friends who live in a bigger town some 30 miles away. Sam and Ben are considered 'children in need' as defined in the 1989 Children Act and the social worker has begun a number of visits to update an assessment of how the children's needs are being met and to monitor the children's welfare and their home environment, both of which have been neglected at times. The social worker knows from the case files that Annette had a disrupted childhood, her name having been put on the child protection register for neglect and she experienced frequent moves. She is estranged from her mother; her father died when she was 11 and she has little contact with extended family.

Regarding her childcare practices, the house shows signs of neglect and there are issues around hygiene: the social worker noticed a pile of dirty nappies heaped up in a corner of the living room. Annette's apparent 'open door' policy results in a number of people coming and going, and on a previous visit the social worker noticed a number of people congregated in the home, two of whom she knew should have been at school. The supervision and some personal care of the children such as feeding and nappy changing appears to be quite disorganised and undertaken by a number of people.

How far does behaviourist theory explain the presenting issues in the case study?

Currently the consequences of Annette's parenting practices are not conditioning her behavioural responses to better meet the needs of her children. The objective of a programme of behaviour modification would be to change this. If Annette disassociated cause and effect in her behaviour, applying the ABC method could address this.

We know Annette had a disrupted childhood and her carers were neglectful in meeting her needs adequately. Social learning theory would suggest she may simply not know how to parent well because she has not experienced this herself and she lacked exposure to good role models to show her how to do this.

In linking thoughts with behaviour, if Annette revealed her 'go to' predominant thought about parenthood is '*I'm no good at being a parent*', this would produce corresponding feelings, physiological reactions and behaviours that would serve to reinforce the predominant thought.

If Annette gave the impression that she was somehow predestined to have an unsupportive partner or fail as a parent, or cannot 'police' who enters her home, then the notion of *learned helplessness* could explain such an absence of any autonomy.

Intervention drawing on ideas from behaviourist theory

The objective of this method of intervention is to address *behaviour*. The first task for the social worker is to decide which of the presenting behaviours described in the case study should be the focus of their intervention. It would make sense to prioritise those behaviours that resulted in the service being necessary, the children being considered '*in need*' (s17 (10) Children Act, 1989) and the agency fulfilling its overarching duty to safeguard and promote the welfare of such children (s17 (1) Children Act, 1989). The Signs of Safety intervention method provides a useful starting point in the question: *What are we worried about?* (see strengths-based approaches).

Any behaviourist intervention requires a detailed quantitative analysis of the presenting issues. Statements in the case study such as '*both of which have been neglected at times*' and '*house shows signs of neglect and there are issues around hygiene*' and '*appears to be quite disorganised*' require a much more precise description, specifying how actual examples of the 'neglect' or disorganisation were manifest. For example, '*on a visit on 19/11/15 at 9.40 am no heating was on in the lounge where the children were. They had nothing on their feet and both their hands and feet were cold to the touch; they had not had breakfast*'. The 'monitoring' would include an evaluation of the frequency of these circumstances, to establish if these were routine.

For the sake of this exercise and brevity, let's assume the social worker had identified the disposal of nappies and Annette undertaking the personal care (feeding and changing) of the children as initial objectives for a programme of behaviour modification (it would be neither ethical nor practical to identify more than two or three objectives to work on at the same time). In applying operant conditioning, careful consideration must be given to how the desired behaviour is going to be reinforced. It needs to be something that Annette values sufficiently to motivate a behavioural change. She could be invited to choose it herself; Annette wants less contact from social care (a negative reinforcement) and a night out without childcare responsibilities (a positive reinforcement). A timescale is agreed over which Annette disposes of the nappies in the bin and undertakes feeding and changing the children. A star chart may be inappropriate due to Annette's age but progress should be recognised with praise. Success breeds confidence and new objectives and reinforcements can be set in train once the initial objectives have been habituated.

If there is evidence that Annette denies or minimises her responsibility, for example, over controlling who enters her house, the antecedent + behaviour = consequence model could be applied to promote the association. In this case, the antecedent (A) of feeling lonely prompts her behaviour (B) of keeping an open door, and produces the consequence (C) that kids use the place to bunk off school. The target for options creation would be to consider ways to obtain more appropriate company.

Applying social learning theory would involve enabling Annette to learn parenting skills by attending parenting classes. This could be reinforced by pro-social modelling through the appointment of a mentor such as a Sure Start volunteer.

In applying CBT the worker would challenge Annette's thought that she is no good at being a parent. It is likely that while there are improvements to be made, some things are working and Annette is fulfilling many parenting tasks adequately or successfully. Holding this mirror image up to Annette would dilute the concentration of the thought, producing less negative feelings etc.

Any evidence of the notion of learned helplessness would need to be challenged in a similar manner by providing contrary evidence of choice and personal responsibility.

Some personal reflections on intervention drawing on ideas from behaviourist theory

Behaviour modification through operant conditioning is a familiar feature; indeed, most of us are subject to it. Your purse or wallet is likely to contain a variety of points-based loyalty cards which serve to modify our consumer behaviour towards particular retailers.

Intervention based on behaviourism is an important tool for the social work practitioner and its techniques work provided intervention is based on accurate analysis and bespoke reinforcements. I have seen operant conditioning used to good effect with people across a broad range of cognitive ability, including adults with a moderate learning disability and with infants in toilet training. The straightforward logic of *we learn what we live* through social learning theory is appealing, especially after the comparative obscurity of Freudian-based theory. CBT enjoys a good empirical research base which bears testament to its efficacy and breadth of application. I have experience of pro-social modelling and mentoring schemes used to provide support to those in the criminal justice system and consider this intervention to be underused.

The interventions on offer though behaviourism have the advantage of being explicable to most and the social worker can have an educative role in explaining the ideas behind the behaviourist techniques they are proposing to use.

Apart from the utility of behaviourist interventions, the discourse they give rise to has profound implications. This is exemplified in the following quote by J B Watson himself in 1925:

Give me a dozen healthy infants, well-formed, and my own special world to bring them up in and I'll guarantee to take any one at random and train him to become any type of specialist I might select – doctor, lawyer, artist, merchant-chief and yes, even beggar-man and thief, regardless of his talents, penchants, tendencies, abilities and vocation and race of his ancestors.

(Parrish, 2014, p 98)

A bold assertion, and perhaps a little dated but its sentiment has up-to-date support in the psychologist Oliver James's recently published book, *Not in Your Genes*, in which he claims that the Human Genome Project has provided evidence of genetic-based variation for some physical characteristics but not significantly so for the differences we see in human psychology. He goes on to assert that the long-established association between heredity and ability is not defensible. This assertion goes to the heart of the nature/nurture debate.

We are accustomed to the notion that the cream will rise to the top and less familiar with its corollary, the sludge will go to the bottom, which despite its unpleasantness is the necessary implication. However, if this is wrong, if 'the cream' enjoy their position through privilege rather than merit then generations have been lost to a lack of will to make serious inroads into inequality and achieving greater social mobility that should result from a greater degree of intolerance to poor nurturing. Mainstream political rhetoric appears not only uncritical but can serve to reconstruct the dissociation between nurture and outcome. For example, Nicky Morgan, the former Secretary of State for Education, in a press release unveiling plans for children's social care reform on 14 January 2016 said, '*We must give every child the best start in life and make sure every child can fulfil their potential – regardless of the circumstances they were born into*'. If, in fact, the circumstances a child is born into dictates, to a significant degree, the extent to which a child is likely to fulfil their potential, such statements are at best fatuous and at worst disingenuous.

References and further reading

BBC News (2016) Bailey Gwynne death: Pupil stabbing death was 'avoidable'. [online] Available at: www.bbc.co.uk/news/uk-scotland-north-east-orkney-shetland-37606361 (accessed 20 February 2017).

Howe, D (2009) *A Brief Introduction to Social Work Theory*. Basingstoke: Palgrave Macmillan.

James, O (2016) *Not in Your Genes*. Vermilion: London.

Morgan, N (2016) *Children's Social Care Reform: Written Statement*. Manchester: Department for Education. [online] Available at: www.parliament.uk/business/publications/written-questions-answers-statements/written-statement/Commons/2016-01-14/HCWS469/ (accessed 20 February 2017).

Williams, C and Garland, A (2002) A Cognitive-Behavioural Therapy Assessment Model for Use in Everyday Clinical Practice. *Advances in Psychiatric Treatment*, 8: 172–9.

SYSTEMS THEORY

Headlines

Nothing exists in isolation but as something in relation to something else.

The behaviour of the individual cannot be understood without reference to the systems to which she or he belongs.

An analysis of the systems to which a person belongs or could access would involve how each part of the system interacts with and impacts on the others.

Intervention is targeted on manipulating these interactions.

One's 'social capital' would be indicative of the complexity or otherwise of our 'social system'.

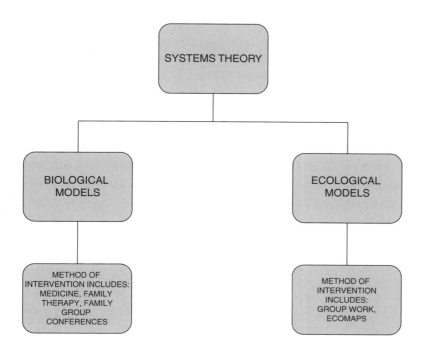

Introduction to systems theory and the difference between biological and ecological models

Malaria is one of the world's most prolific and dangerous diseases and is proving a very complex problem to control. There are attempts to control it by attacking vulnerable points in the breeding cycle of the mosquito, which are biological as they concern the carrier organism itself. There are attempts to control it by considering the predators the adult mosquito has and promoting their numbers; this is an ecological intervention as it concerns relationships between organisms. An application of the first example was tried early on in the fight against malaria. The larvae of the mosquito are born in water but 'breathe' air, gaining access to this by being suspended from the water's surface tension. Break this 'skin' on the water's surface and the larvae sinks and drowns. Detergent breaks the surface water tension; hence spraying large areas of swampy terrain with detergent was a method initially used to reduce the number of mosquitos. Dragonflies are one of the natural predators of mosquitos. Dragonfly larvae use the same method of being water born and suspended by the surface tension of the water to breathe so using detergent to reduce the number of mosquitos resulted in a similar reduction in the number of dragonflies. Some fish and birds are natural predators of mosquitos but are also reliant on a number of other insects in their diet which use the same method of respiration in their larvae stage. So in using one crude attempt to kill mosquitos, a whole complex **system** of food chains and webs was disrupted.

The human body is comprised of a number of systems, for example, the nervous system, the respiratory system and the endocrine system to name but a few. Medical interventions and treatments seek to change how these systems work, both within themselves and their intra-relationships with other systems. In human anatomy these systems could be dissected out of the whole body, which would illustrate the common properties of systems: they serve a function and so can said to be *goal-orientated*; they are bounded so we can know what is 'inside' and what lies 'outside' a particular system; it can be said that the sum of the whole appears greater than the sum of its parts. Social workers, while not in any sense medically trained, should not discount or lose sight of the possibility of medical interventions being legitimate and appropriate in certain circumstances.

A definition of systems theory could look like this:

A social system is a system of processes of interaction between actors ... it is the structure of the relations between the actors as involved in the interactive process which is essentially the structure of the social system. The system is a network of such relationships.

(Parsons, 1991, p 15)

A social-work-related example of an application of systems theory can be found in Eileen Munro's *Review of Child Protection* (2010), part 1 of which was entitled 'A systems analysis'. She explains why a systems analysis was used in her review in paragraph 1.1:

> A systems approach will help this review to avoid looking at parts of the child protection system in isolation, and to analyse how the system functions as a whole.

(Munro, 2010, p 10)

Social workers should be well versed in an ecological model that was originally introduced in 2000, namely The Framework for the Assessment of Children in Need and their Families and currently known as the Assessment Framework through Working Together 2015 (Department for Education, 2015).

The framework represents the child's world and has three *domains*, namely: the child's developmental needs, parenting capacity and family and environmental factors, within which 20 'dimensions' are embedded.

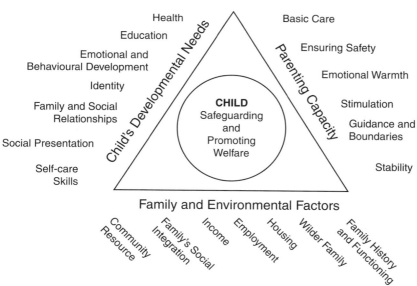

Figure 2.4 Ecological models; the Assessment Framework (Department for Education, 2015, p 22)

Uri Bronfenbrenner developed another ecological model to illustrate the spheres of influence as represented by family, cultural and societal systems generationally, which is shown in Figure 2.5.

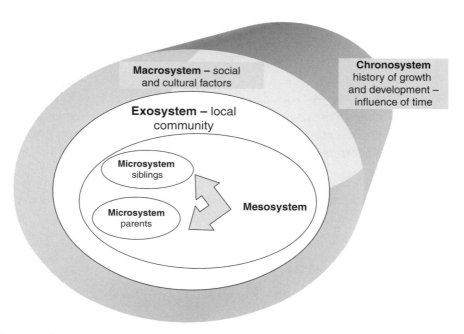

Figure 2.5 Bronfenbrenner's ecological systems model
(Bronfenbrenner, 1979, cited in Crawford and Walker, 2014, p 26)

Neither model provides any qualitative information about the amount of stimulation a parent might give a particular child or the predominant dynamic in a sibling microsystem but they provide a structure by which such features of one's upbringing could be *systematically* enquired into. Such an enquiry is comprised of two parts; firstly, the information-gathering phase and secondly, the analysis of what this actually means for the individual concerned.

There has been more information gathered about Jimmy and his home circumstances. Figure 2.6 identifies the members of his immediate family, and the statements which follow are a selection of comments made including fact and opinion that offer insights into the nature of the relationships Jimmy has with his family.

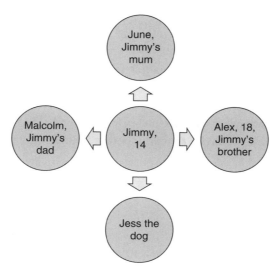

Figure 2.6 Analyses of families as systems

June has limited mobility due to rheumatoid arthritis; although not her carer as such, Jimmy helps his mum with household tasks and does some shopping.

Jimmy worries about his mum and is aware her condition impacts on the quality of her life and is painful.

Malcolm works at a local food processing factory. He is unsympathetic towards June and her condition, regarding it as burdensome on the family's functioning.

Alex works at the same place as his dad. They enjoy a good relationship, occasionally having a pint at the pub together. They both have fair hair.

An education welfare officer visited Jimmy's parents to discuss his school attendance. June was quiet but Malcolm was forthright in expressing his opinion that education had not done him much good and was dismissive of its importance for Jimmy.

June used to walk Jess when she could but from the age of 11 Jimmy took this on and thought of her as his dog. Sadly, when Jimmy was 13 she developed an infection in her leg. Unknown to Jimmy, his dad took her to the vet to have her put down rather than for treatment, later saying cost had been the deciding factor.

Jimmy looks forward to seeing his uncle Dave who lives with his wife Anne and two daughters in a rural village some five miles away. During the summer holidays, Dave took Jimmy on a few jobs to farms to help him in his work as an agricultural equipment mechanic.

An analysis of this information reveals some tension in the marital relationship, and between Jimmy and his dad who Jimmy regards as uncaring and cruel and he remains resentful over Jess. Jimmy cares about his mum and wishes her life was easier for her. Jimmy has a good relationship with his uncle. He does not feel he has much in common with his brother but this does not appear to bother Jimmy.

Application of systems theory in social work practice

Applying systems theory in social work practice involves bringing about change through manipulating the systems, their relationships with the individual and others and inter-relationships between systems, the individual and others. They might already be within the system, their family for example, or could be introduced to and included in a system, such as the mentoring scheme previously discussed.

Factual circumstances are not usually amenable to change, but how we think and feel about them can change. We have seen through psycho-dynamic intervention that *the self* is the target for change, whereas in behaviourism, one's behaviour is the target for change. However, with systems theory, intervention can be less personal; the target for change is a system that could be once or more removed from the individual concerned. For example, an assessment of support for June under the Care Act 2014 resulted in the provision of help for June, which had the knock-on effect of reducing some of the stress in the marital relationship and made Jimmy feel better about his mum as she was getting some help.

Further examples of systems intervention with Jimmy could include his involvement in a dog-walking scheme that not only brought him into contact with dogs but provided some additional pocket money. Furthermore, the education welfare officer arranged for a careers adviser to take Jimmy on a visit to the local agricultural college where he learnt about courses and admission requirements. Using the example of Jimmy and some basic information about his family serves as a brief introduction to the application of systems theory. An application in practice would require some direct work with Jimmy to discover the systems pertinent to him and their spheres of influence before undertaking any manipulation of those that already exist or introducing new ones. The tools commonly used in direct work to explore these 'spheres' are genograms and ecomaps.

Genograms and ecomaps

As with many forms of social work intervention, careful regard should be given to the emotional content that can be realised and released through exploring feelings and relationships using these tools. A rapport and ideally a relationship needs to be established before such work is utilised to enable the service user to feel sufficiently 'safe' to explore such work and to benefit from any support the social worker may provide in helping the service user undertake this work.

Family therapy, family group conferences and group work

Families are systems and the individuals that comprise them take on roles. These *roles* may be perceived by the individual and by other members of the family but the *perceptions* can be similar or very different. A family therapist would seek to explore these and bring differing perceptions to the awareness of the family members, within the context that no one family member is 'to blame' for the manner in which the family functions as a whole. It requires specific skills in therapy and counselling, beyond that usually acquired through qualifying as a social worker but these could be gained though developing a practice specialism and training.

Family group conferences (FGCs) appeared as a feature of social work practice in the UK following New Zealand introducing the Children, Young Persons and Their Families Act 1989 at the same time as the Children Act 1989 became the primary piece of civil child welfare legislation in England and Wales. The New Zealand practice model sought to both empower family members and encourage them to take responsibility where there was a risk of statutory intervention by the state as a result of concern for the welfare of children and/or receiving them into their care. It is important to stress that the family group conference was not a substitute for statutory intervention where necessary, but by law, an FGC would have to have taken place prior to such intervention to explore and give the family/extended family the opportunity to ameliorate or resolve the concerns and thus render statutory intervention unnecessary.

The law in England and Wales stopped short of making a similar statutory requirement but adopted the model as a practice initiative that demonstrated tangible partnership working. In keeping with this philosophy, many local authorities employed suitable people, independent from their social services departments, to chair the FGC who ran the meetings in a manner that conferred the responsibility for decision-making to the family members. The 'professionals' such as social workers were to be available as a resource to be used at the behest of the family. Who constituted *the family* was for its members to define and could include both biologically and non-biologically related persons. The chair would assist the family with co-ordination, planning who was doing what and reviewing the plan.

Groups are systems and group work can be an empowering method of intervention, bringing people together with circumstances, experiences, interests or a goal in common with a view to sharing these experiences in a group rather than individually. Group work can be facilitated by skilled helper but is usually intended to be egalitarian in nature, where the 'benefit' of membership is for the group's participants to define. Outcomes will to some extent depend on the nature of the group and its objectives but an example might be a group for women who have experienced domestic abuse. Such a group could be facilitated by a female domestic-abuse project worker and would meet for a limited number of occasions. Anticipated benefits for its members might be gaining confidence in the knowledge that the issues they faced alone such as remaining in the relationship through love or wanting to keep their family together were not unique to them.

Effective group facilitation is a skill that a social worker could develop as a practice specialism. Groups are considered to have a life cycle of their own but have 'stages' in common. One of the important skills of a group facilitator is to help the group to manage these stages and their transitions. A number of commentators have identified these stages but Tuckman's work is noteworthy in defining five stages:

Forming, where the group's membership is established.

Storming, where the 'getting to know you' of the group's members occurs in which allegiances and tensions within relationships develop.

Norming, where the group acclimatises to and accommodates its differences and in a general sense 'gels'.

Performing, where the group orientates itself to the common purpose or task it has formed to address.

Adjourning, where the group dissembles having achieved its objectives.

(Tuckman, 1965, cited in Teater, 2014, p 244)

Let's again return to the case study we are using to show how theory offers an explanation and a method of intervention. The details are essentially the same but we now know a little more about Annette to better understand her systems.

Case study

Annette is a white 23-year-old woman with two children: a baby, Sam, aged 18 months, and a toddler, Ben, aged two and a half. They live in a small rural town. Her current partner, Andy, is an intravenous drug user who lives part of the time at Annette's; the rest of the time he spends at friends who live in a bigger town some 30 miles away. Sam and Ben are considered 'children in need' as defined in the 1989 Children Act. There is concern regarding the extent to which the children's needs are being met and their environment cared for, both of which have been neglected at times. The supervision of the children appears quite disorganised and is undertaken by a number of people. The social worker is concerned for the development of their attachment to a primary carer.

The social worker knows from the case files that Annette had a disrupted childhood, her name having been put on the child protection register for neglect and she experienced frequent moves. She is estranged from her mother, her father died when she was 11 and she has little contact with extended family, which comprise a maternal grandmother and step-grandfather, a brother, sister, nephew and niece. Regarding friends, Annette said they were difficult to keep and maintain contact with due to the frequent moves but there were two significant ones she remembered, Rachel and Joanne, but they have lost contact now. The social worker knows a little more about Annette; Ben's father is Mark but he has no contact with Annette or Ben. Andy is Sam's father.

School was important to Annette; she enjoyed reading and some sports activities including swimming. Regarding work, she had jobs in the retail trade and misses the contact she had with people, as all she sees now is the HV, and loan collection worker. She appears quite lethargic and confesses to feeling quite low and 'cannot be bothered' at times, the 'open door' being an example; anyway, it's company and the young people play with the kids. She considers herself to be overweight and is not comfortable with her body image. Regarding Andy, she knows he does not offer her much by way of useful support but offers her some companionship on occasion.

How far does systems theory explain the presenting issues in the case study?

There are some inherent assumptions in all theoretical frameworks. The main assumption in systems theory is that there is an association between the extent to which a person is integrated or has some connection with their social world and their sense of well-being. More specifically, isolation and disconnectedness is likely to foster a poor sense of well-being and is likely to adversely affect functioning, and a rich network of integration and connectedness is likely to foster a good, healthy sense of well-being, enhancing functioning. There is one rider to this assumption and that is that there is a qualitative element to the degree of connectedness or social capital one could draw on, and this is perhaps more important than any quantitative measure. For example, with the advent of social media someone could boast 1500 'friends' on Facebook but have no intimate or significant relationships.

In respect of Annette, she has two children who will be needy and demanding of her but she has very few sources of support and social opportunities that could meet her needs as a young woman. In some respects her world has 'shrunk' compared to what it was like when she was at school and when she worked. So this is how systems theory may explain her low mood and lack of motivation, the association between this and her poor connectivity to a social world.

Intervention drawing on the ideas from systems theory

The objective of this method of intervention would be to firstly establish an understanding of Annette's current 'systems' and their relative value to her, and then to explore what changes she would like to make to her existing systems and what new or re-discovered systems she would like to have in her world. A starting point with this work may be to use the 'tools' discussed earlier, the genogram and the ecomap. The genogram would provide a vehicle for establishing Annette's *family tree* whereas the ecomap could help to establish Annette's social world and the significance to her of the parts that comprised it. This work could develop into an exploration of what she would like to have in her life and if and how these could become a feature of her world. For example, the following areas could be explored:

a. Her relationship with Andy and if she is satisfied with the degree of contact and level of support he offers her; this could develop into some direct work with Andy in respect of the relationship he has with Annette, Sam and Ben.

b. The circumstances of the 'estrangement' with her mum and if she would like this to be different.

c. What she remembers of her father and the significance she attached to this loss.

d. What of the members of her extended family and if there is anyone she would like to establish contact with.

e. She identified two former friends as being significant, Rachel and Joanne. Would there be something to be gained by trying to re-establish contact through social media?

f. The role Mark played in her life and if she would like him to have contact with Ben.

g. Annette enjoyed reading – does she still read? What access to reading material does she have? Is she a member of the library and the toy library for the kids?

h. Annette also enjoyed sports, notably swimming – does she still swim? Could she join the local sports centre? Exercise helps to keep weight down and is good for mental health.

i. Annette enjoyed her retail work and the contact with people it brought. Could she undertake some part-time shop work while the kids were in nursery a couple of days a week? Would she consider voluntary work in a charity shop as a way to get back into it?

j. Annette says she is not comfortable with her body image. How might she feel better about this? She might reframe her idea about body image or be willing to look at her diet. If she was interested in receiving support for dieting she could join a local Weight Watchers group.

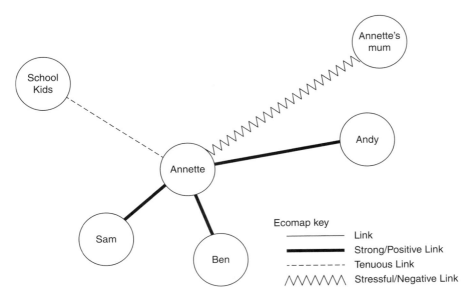

Figure 2.7 Annette's ecomap at first meeting

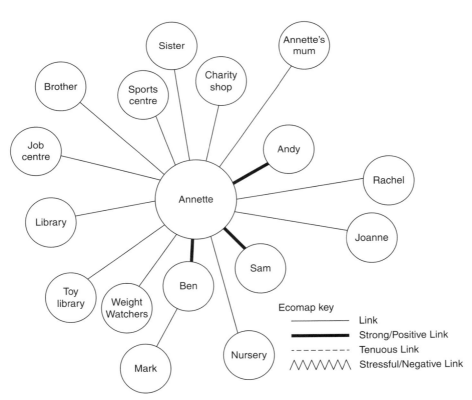

Figure 2.8 Annette's ecomap following the application of system's theory and direct work undertaken with Annette aimed at developing her relationships and interests

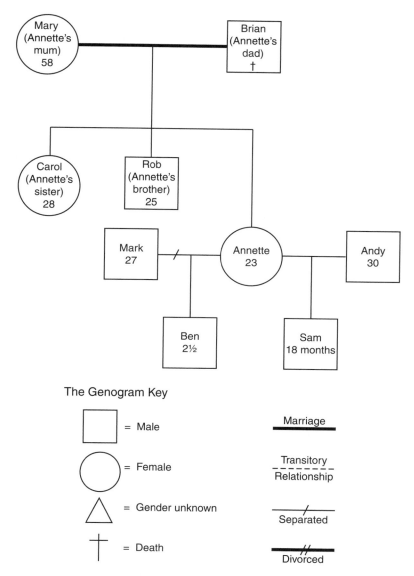

The Genogram Key

☐ = Male

○ = Female

△ = Gender unknown

† = Death

━━━ Marriage

----- Transitory Relationship

━/━ Separated

━//━ Divorced

Figure 2.9 Annette's genogram

Other interventions using systems could include recognition that lethargy and low mood may indicate depression, which can be treated with CBT but may also benefit from medication. Furthermore, being overweight may indicate an underactive thyroid so suggesting Annette sees her GP may be appropriate.

Family therapy usually lends itself to intervention where there are more than two cogent family members. However, a family group conference may offer a means to mobilise support from the extended family if initial enquiries as to preparedness to become involved looked promising.

Group work could be utilised by inviting young mums on the estate to come together with an interest in common, for example, enquiring into what community resources they would find most beneficial – eg setting up a child sitting circle or a service users' group? A facilitator, venue and a crèche would need to be provided for the group.

Some personal reflections drawing on the ideas from systems theory

You might be thinking, all well and good but what about the presenting issues that led to Sam and Ben being children in need? At what point is the social worker going to address the quality of childcare and supervision? The answer is on a needs basis but reference to this, if necessary, is not the primary target of intervention using systems theory. The benefit of such intervention to Sam and Ben is essentially a by-product of enabling Annette to feel better about herself as a person, a woman and a mum by improving the extent to which her needs are met by improving her social systems and networks. The priority for the social worker has not changed – it remains the children's welfare – but bringing about improvements for them is realised by bringing about improvements in the sense of well-being of their carer. In this sense, intervention using systems theory can feel less threatening to the service user's persona than some other interventions. The method of intervention requires careful and considered analysis of how the systems concerned could be manipulated to produce the most beneficial effect, which depends on the work undertaken with the service user exploring this. Proposed changes to systems need to be achievable, affordable and subject to review.

Group work can be a powerful tool to raise awareness, combat isolation and boost self-worth and esteem. As a social work intervention, I consider it to be underutilised as the method falls outside of the traditional *casework* model which has come to dominate social work practice. It may suit social workers wishing to promote and mobilise the strengths of service users as effective group work often involves some devolution of power from 'the professionals' to the users of the service.

The use of family group conferences also involves some devolution of power from 'the professionals' to the 'family' group members but it is not a substitute for initial child protection conferences where the level of concern for the welfare of the child warrants such a meeting. In these situations, the local safeguarding children's board procedures apply.

References and further reading

Care Act 2014 (c.23) (2014) London: TSO. [online] Available at: www.legislation.gov.uk/ukpga/2014/23/contents/enacted (accessed 23 March 2017).

Crawford, K and Walker, J (2014) *Social Work and Human Development*. London: Learning Matters.

Children, Young Persons, and Their Families Act 1989 (1989) Wellington, New Zealand: Parliamentary Counsel Office. [online] Available at: www.legislation.govt.nz/act/public/1989/0024/latest/DLM147088.html (accessed 23 March 2017).

Department for Education (2015) *Working Together to Safeguard Children: A Guide to Inter-agency Working to Safeguard and Promote the Welfare of Children*. Manchester: Department for Education. [online] Available at: www.gov.uk/government/uploads/system/uploads/attachment_data/file/419595/Working_Together_to_Safeguard_Children.pdf (accessed 23 March 2017).

Munro, E (2010) *The Munro Review of Child Protection*. Manchester: Department for Education. [online] Available at: www.gov.uk/government/uploads/system/uploads/attachment_data/file/175407/TheMunro Review-Part_one.pdf (accessed 23 March 2017).

Parsons, T (1991) *Social System*. London: Routledge.

Teater, B (2014) *An Introduction to Applying Social Work Theories and Methods*. Maidenhead: Open University Press; McGraw Hill Education. [A thorough exposition of group work could merit a book in its own right but a useful introduction can be found in Chapter 14.]

RADICAL/STRUCTURAL THEORY

Headlines

People's problems do not arise from their innate characteristics or personality. Their source is the result of the way society is structured which favours some and disadvantages others.

Society is deliberately structured in a way to both establish and perpetuate inequality by the powerful and those in whose interest it is to replicate the dominant hegemony in that society.

Action under the banner of radical/structural analysis involves challenging the normative power structures in society.

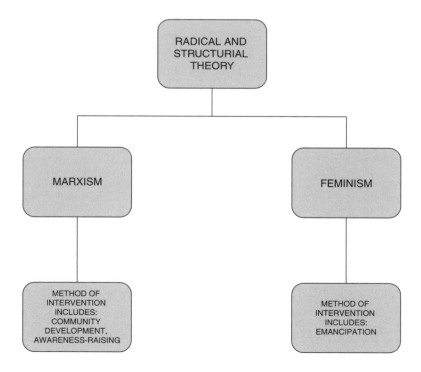

Introductory overview of radical/ structural theory

As psycho-dynamic theory is all about the inner world and internal processes, radical/structural theory takes the opposite position. An individual's personality and traits do not feature as the cause for the type of person they have become. In a radical and structural theory of explanation, cause is found in an analysis of society's structures and the extent to which they promote or hamper life chances, social mobility, social capital and fulfilling one's potential (what Abraham Maslow described as '*self-actualisation*' in his hierarchy of needs), for the people who comprise that society. It follows that any such analysis will involve the role that privilege and advantage and those of deprivation, poverty, oppression and discrimination play in affording those life chances and establishing a society in which equality of opportunity is created for all its members.

Radical social work theory is critical of traditional casework which, it argues, pathologises people's problems as the emphasis is placed on the individual, disguising their true cause of structural disadvantage. At a societal level, the effect of placing the emphasis of causation of society's ills such as crime, poverty, drug use, violence, teenage pregnancy, obesity etc on the individual results in accepting the causes of such ills being solely to do with the individual, rather than a consequence of the way society is structured. Such acceptance becomes habituated as natural and inevitable as people are socialised into society, which is an example of the hegemony previously referred to. An example of this analysis is given in the verse of a popular hymn: 'All Things Bright and Beautiful'; the original version contained the following:

The rich man in his castle.
The poor man at his gate,
He (God) made them, high or lowly,
And ordered their estate.

(Alexander, 1850)

The assertion that inequality is ordained rather than socially constructed presents such social divisions based on class and privilege as so evidently manifest in the TV series *Downton Abbey* not only acceptable but as corresponding to a 'natural order', critics of which are cast as motivated by envy.

Although many sociologists, research foundations and Trusts have made significant contributions to an understanding of such an analysis, any introduction to this field would have to start with its founder, the analytical social historian and philosopher

Karl Marx (1818–1883) who, in collaboration with Friedrich Engels, developed a social theory of Marxism which considered capitalism to be fundamentally divisive and ultimately a transitory phase of social evolution. Marx held that the way in which societies organise the manufacture and distribution of the goods and services the people in that society need will primarily shape the lives of people and provide the '*lived experience*' of those in that society. Marx's lifelong work (he famously spent his latter years living in London, studying at the British Library) is, irrespective of one's political stance, an erudite and complex body of work.

Reference to Marx's work in this book can only offer the most rudimentary outline as it is a body of study in its own right. However, the basic idea may be revealed through the industrial disputes which were rife during part of Edward Heath's Conservative prime ministership of 1970–74 and resulted in a three-day working week (Worthington, 2014) and the downfall of that government. Margaret Thatcher appeared determined to achieve a different outcome during her premiership of the Conservative government of 1979–90 in the way she managed a dispute with workers in the coal mining industry in the 1980s (Stacey, 2014). This very bitter dispute eventually resulted in defeat for the miners' union and a decimated coal mining industry. A more recent example would include what happened to British Home Stores, the retail chain owned by Philip Green, knighted for his services to retailing. Green allegedly drained it of capital, leaving its workers' pension fund insolvent, and sold the chain for £1.00 to a two-times bankrupt businessman. The chain subsequently went into receivership, leaving its 11,000 workforce jobless while Sir Philip lounged on his multimillion pound yacht (*BBC News*, 2016).

A Marxist analysis of such examples would reveal what is claimed as the true nature of capitalist society: a conflictual relationship between the owners and controllers of the means of production (the bourgeoisie) and the workers (the proletariat) in which the former exploit the latter. In such disputes the thin veneer of consensus is splintered, revealing the warring factions of opposed interests. Marx envisaged that eventually this antagonistic social system, which produces such inequality, would be replaced with a more collectivist system of socialism or communism. Critics of such (proposed) social systems argue that these have already been tried and failed, resulting in totalitarian regimes that give rise to oppressive dictators. They regard the concepts of self-interest and personal agency as praiseworthy, motivating forces for individuals and the resulting competition between them is considered healthy, producing what people want in a lean and efficient way. (Personal agency here means the subjective sense of being in control of initiating and executing decisions independently. The extent to which one can genuinely achieve this is contested between the political right who advocate individualism and the political left who stress the interdependency of social systems and argue that personal agency is illusionary).

Advocates for socialism stress the requirement of an international nature of such a system and argue that the totalitarian states seen in Stalin's USSR and Mao's China were not examples of socialism. They argue the stress on individualism in capitalist societies justifies the politics of greed and that capitalism's need for continued growth through obsolescence and consumerism is wasteful, competition is divisive and conceals the interdependence any functioning society relies on. For example, consider the pay-as-you-earn (PAYE) taxation system in the UK. It is not hypothecated. Current earners pay the current old age pension bill, irrespective of what the current old age pensioners have saved or how long they live. Current earners pay for education irrespective of whether or not they have children. Current earners fund welfare benefits for the unemployed and for those who cannot work through disability. Current earners fund the NHS irrespective of their health.

It is difficult to envisage or establish a middle way between these opposing perspectives on how people should live that has authenticity, hence the *right* and *left* political debate continues as to which better serves humanity.

A radical analysis is not solely concerned with the means of production and economics. It can be applied wherever the normative or the usual standard of how power is exercised can be challenged. So Marxism is an example of radical theory, as is feminism, which challenges the dominance of men and the ways they oppress women. Other examples may include: the Greenham Common peace movement in which women protested about the presence of nuclear weapons in the UK; so-called *eco-warriors* who set up camp in trees earmarked to be felled to make way for a new motorway; people blocking the road protesting about the transport of livestock for slaughter.

The 'action' taken under a radical banner includes protest marches and non-violent civil disobedience but may extend to being illegal, which invites the criticism that the law and its makers enforce and maintain the established power relations. Whether or not such action is moral is dependent on whose perspective is taken. The extreme example of a person sending a bomb in the post to a scientist who performs experiments on live animals is certainly illegal and morally questionable but not to the antivivisectionist protestor who posts it. A less contentious example of radical action has been the campaign led by some with physical disabilities to request facilities to enable their participation in society to be integral to building design and urban planning. A few wheelchair users chaining themselves together across a busy main road brought attention to their fight for kerb drops, ramps, lifts and toilets they can use and contributed to an effective and ultimately successful campaign.

Radical/structural theory, and social work

The relationship between radical/structural theory and social work is not an easy one, perhaps the best word to describe the relationship is *ambiguous*. The reason for this is found in the dynamic between the aims of social work and some of the methods of intervention used to achieve them. Chapter 1 introduced the international definition of social work as approved by the IFSW General Meeting and the IASSW General Assembly in July 2014, which states:

Social work is a practice-based profession and an academic discipline that promotes social change and development, social cohesion, and the empowerment and liberation of people. Principles of social justice, human rights, collective responsibility and respect for diversities are central to social work. Underpinned by theories of social work, social sciences, humanities and indigenous knowledge, social work engages people and structures to address life challenges and enhance wellbeing.

The aims of promoting social change and development, social cohesion, and the empowerment and liberation of people could not be advanced without reference to the socio-political environment in which people live their lives and the advocacy of those who are less powerful and disadvantaged. While the users of social services are varied, they are likely to be those who are less powerful and disadvantaged and this is borne out in the number of service users whose main source of income is derived from state benefits. Social workers may recognise the discrimination and oppression their service users may have been and continue to be subject to but how might such recognition be made manifest in their practice? At an intellectual level, they may consciously adhere to values that do not add to the discrimination and oppression their service users suffer but ultimately local authority social workers are organs of the State. If they are engaged with an involuntary service user in upholding the rights of those in the care of the service user, the intervention undertaken may not only feel oppressive for the service user but be necessarily so if improvements in the quality of care of the *primary* service user are to be made. For example, the carer of an elderly person is physically abusing and neglecting them. It is the task of the adult safeguarding team to intervene. The carer might not welcome such intervention, and find it oppressive, but their intervention is justified in coming to the aid of the elderly person who is their primary service user.

The dynamic has resulted in a critique of social work intervention that basically charges social work as being allied to 'oiling the wheels' of the very system it should be fighting against on behalf of its service users. This critique was more prevalent in

the 1960s and 1970s and was exemplified in the Case Con movement and its mani-
festo of 1975 (see appendix in Bailey and Brake, 1975). The critique argued that the
only form of intervention untainted by the charge was that which aimed to stimulate
community development and that traditional *casework* did little to improve the lives
of the service users subject to it, as it failed to address the fundamental inequalities
the service users are subject to.

Although such arguments remain at a philosophical level, they do not feature as
much as they did within the discourse of social work education and practice. There
may be several reasons for this: there are fewer jobs in community development for
social workers than there used to be; the 'subject' of social class seems to have given
way to an emphasis being placed on the way we regard our fellow citizens as in anti-
discriminatory thoughts and actions; the argument itself seems somehow 'old hat'
despite the continuing inequality in society; perhaps a political career is best suited
to take the argument forward, as there is little a social worker can actually *do* about
the structural inequality a particular service user is considered subject to.

Finally, we cannot ignore the incidence in which parent A neglects their child whereas
parent B does not, despite their having had very similar life chances. This does not
justify inequality but it does herald consideration of the emotional context of people's lives, which radical and structural analysis takes little account of in terms of
causation but would highlight the impact of the effect of long-term grinding poverty
and being *at the bottom of the pile* would have on one's self-concept of status, self-
esteem and well-being.

This book is about theory and its application and does not have the remit to develop
the case for or against structural inequality. There are some sources of information
with which to consider the evidence for this at the end of the chapter. However, there
is one research finding that is of interest in respect of social mobility in which the UK
continues to rank low. Parental occupation remains the best indicator for predicting
the occupational status of children. In 2005 the Sutton Trust commissioned a report
by Blanden and Machin on recent changes in intergenerational mobility in the UK.
Their findings allude to the effect of the influence aspiration may play even when set
against ability. The study found a fall in intergenerational mobility for children born
in the UK in 1970 compared with those born in 1958. This revealed that the adult
earnings of the 1970 cohort were more closely linked to the income of their parents
when compared with those in the 1958 cohort. Most notably, the proportion of people from the poorest fifth of families obtaining a degree increased from 5 per cent to
7 per cent, while the graduation rates for the richest fifth rose from 20 per cent to
37 per cent.

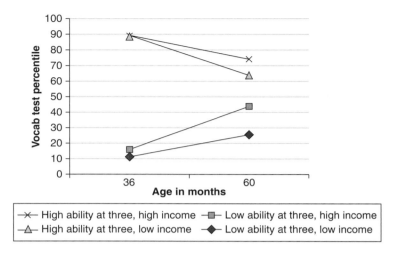

Figure 2.10 Evolution of test scores by ability grouping and family income for children in the millennium cohort study

This means the gap in test scores between high-achieving children from poor backgrounds and low-achieving children from affluent backgrounds has shrunk from more than 70 percentiles at age three to 20 percentiles by age five. If this trend were to continue, the children from affluent backgrounds would be likely to overtake the poorer children in test scores before age seven. (Blandin and Machin, 2007, p 23)

Application of radical/structural theory to social work practice

The methods of intervention in social work that are most congruent with radical or structural theory are those which seek to make improvements in the lives of groups and communities. Consequently, community development project work and various forms of advocacy for service-user groups are the methods of intervention most associated with radical or structural theory. The role of the social worker in community development is that of initiator/facilitator. An example of a project would be a campaign to improve the insulation in an estate of ageing council housing. A project might take several years to come to fruition and begin with liaising with members or leaders of the community to establish a need. In the example given, this may involve liaising with members of a tenants' association. If one does not already exist, the first task would be to leaflet the estate inviting interest in developing one. The tenants' association would canvass opinion to identify a campaign issue. The tenants cite the biggest problem with their housing is that the homes are difficult and expensive to heat, prone to condensation, causing damp due to their prefabricated concrete construction and poor quality insulation. The campaign is launched, tenants' meetings are scheduled, a committee formed with the aim of lobbying the district council to upgrade the insulation in their housing stock on the estate.

It is important that the ownership of such projects remains with the community – it is their campaign and not the social worker's. In fact, the social worker might play a part in the early identification and organisation of the initiative, providing access to some administrative tasks such as the production of leaflets and facilitating group work skills in helping with the formation of a committee but once it's up and running their role becomes minimal and they may even withdraw. It is easy to see why social worker posts for community development work are uncommon in a time of financial restraint. In a unitary authority, for example, the authority would employ the social worker who may be facilitating a group whose aims result in increasing that authority's expenditure. Because of this 'political' dimension and potential for a conflict of interest, much of the employment for jobs whose role is to advocate for specific interest groups, NAYPIC (National Association for Young People in Care) for example, are held within the private and voluntary sector. Central government might help fund such organisations with a grant and local authorities might commission their services but it may be apposite to avoid employing people to advocate for those they have responsibilities to provide services for.

Let's see how we might apply radical/structural theory to the case study we are working with.

Case study

Annette is a white 23-year-old woman with two children: a baby, Sam, aged 18 months and a toddler, Ben, aged two and a half. Sam and Ben are considered 'children in need' as defined in the 1989 Children Act and there are concerns for the children's welfare in terms of some neglect issues and poor supervision. Andy is still on the scene but offers Annette little in terms of support and helping her with the children. In fact, he is critical of her and describes her as lazy and overweight. He considers her responsible for social services being involved despite being the father of one of the children and is adding to the social worker's concern by using intravenous drugs on the premises. Annette's social worker is from the children and family's team, and is updating an assessment of how the needs of the children are being met.

However, the social worker is mindful of the broader social conditions in which Annette and the children live, and questions the style of traditional casework that has a tendency to pathologise service users and ignores the structural discrimination that so often characterises them and defines their lives. This seems to make sense as Annette lives on a street particularly noted for 'problem families' and is noticeably run down on an estate that has a high proportion of social housing; households headed by single parents and whose main source of income is welfare benefits. The estate is considered to be in an area of economic deprivation. The social worker is aware that colleagues from the family-support team visit two other families on the same street.

On today's visit the social worker notes that the children are in pants and vests; their hands and feet are cold to the touch. In the living room there is a one-bar electric fire that is on but the house feels cold and damp. The social worker has discussed this with the district council who explained that the houses in the row where Annette lives were built with prefabricated concrete blocks. An adviser from Shelter has said this type of house construction has very little thermal insulation and is difficult and expensive to heat. During the visit, someone knocks on the door. Annette takes £5 from her purse and gives it to the woman who has called. Annette explains that she took out a £200 loan through Shop-a-Cheque, a money loan company, so as to give the children a good Christmas and she has to pay it off over three years. The social worker asks the rate of interest on the loan; Annette seems unsure as to what this is. The social worker is aware that there are several women with children in the local neighbourhood who appear to have similar issues in common and who might benefit from meeting up, but they have young children and childcare provision is expensive.

The social worker might make sure that Annette is claiming all the welfare benefits she is entitled to and discuss with her the interest she might pay, for example, at an APR of 28.7% (not uncommonly high) she would pay £423.36 back on a £200.00 loan over three years. The social worker could consider the use of a Home-Start or woman's aid volunteer, not to replace the social worker but to support Annette as the focus, which is not the role for the social worker whose focus must remain the welfare of the children.

But what might social work that solely adopts a radical, structural method of intervention look like in the broadest terms? There is quite a lot a community development worker could do given a mandate.

Emancipation would be a key objective. This could be in terms of awareness-raising in relation to social class and equality of opportunities, income distribution and taxation, health and longevity. It could also address, perhaps with some justification, the usefulness of some men, to some women, from a radical feminist perspective. This could be explored through a women's group. A community development project worker could campaign for: the need for a community centre on the estate, with provision for a crèche to enable a woman's group to meet and a toy library; a safe playground with a paid assistant on the estate; a programme of upgrading the insulation of the housing stock; the creation of a credit union which charges considerably less interest than that of loan companies.

Intervention drawing on the ideas from radical/structural theory

Structural discrimination and the way it manifests itself in terms of life chances and social inclusion or exclusion is very real and can offer an explanation for the presenting issues we see in the case study of Annette, her children and many families like them. Awareness-raising in terms of structural discrimination and a historic appreciation of male oppression and how it might function in some relationships has an important role to play. A community development worker has the mandate to address issues affecting the community. The social worker allocated to Annette is from the children and families team and in supervision, the social worker's manager would want to hear of the progress being achieved in the quality of childcare practices rather than any progress being made in the emancipation of Annette. Consequently, there are limitations for the application of radical/structural theory in case studies like the one we are using. Annette and Andy may well have received minimal input in terms of enhancing their life chances and compared with many may be relatively powerless. The difficulty is that Sam and Ben are less powerful than Annette and Andy and have to rely on them to meet their needs. Issues regarding life chances and social inclusion or exclusion are very real but so is having cold hands and feet, the hygiene risks from the dirty nappies and the consequences of neglect and poor attachment. These children have not got the time to wait for structural inequalities to be eradicated so some direct work will be necessary, however stigmatising and oppressive it might be. Being a victim of severe or persistent neglect is also oppressive!

Some personal reflections on intervention drawing from the ideas of radical/structural theory

I was a mature student when I enrolled to qualify as a social worker and the decision to do so was, in part, a political one. I felt the values I held were more attuned to those social work stood for, more so than other occupations I had tried. I was exposed to the suspicion with which some members of the public view social work and the motivations of its workers early in my training. As a student project a group of us were tasked to undertake some social research on a housing estate. As this was situated some distance from where we were studying, we rented a room for a day per week for the term. This was purely a commercial arrangement, renting a room in a house that happened to be managed by a women's group. However, when they learnt that those using the room were trainee social workers they withdrew the rental agreement. This disquieting experience forced us to consider how the role of social worker was perceived and wrested us from the somewhat naïve, loosely described motivation as 'wanting to help' and the assumption that this would be taken at face value.

Nevertheless, I undertook my first placement as a community development worker, which I found an authentic role, although on other placements I came to see the merit in relationship-based intervention and change. However, I continued to be persuaded by the soundness of the arguments radical/structural analysis makes regarding how privilege and consequently disadvantage are constructed and perpetuated and remain so. However, I do not look to social work to seriously challenge this, while services are arranged and delivered to individuals. Perhaps this would be different were the *primary service user* defined as the community. I do not intend to suggest that the social worker may dismiss the structural discrimination and disadvantage their service users have suffered or are subject to. On the contrary, they need to be mindful of it but not be disarmed by it as there will be no substitute for the need for the children and families social worker to say '*Let's get some socks on Sam and Ben's feet.*'

References and further reading

Alexander, C (1850) *Hymns for Little Children*. Philadelphia, USA: Herman Hooker.

Bailey, R and Brake, M (1975) *Radical Social Work*. London: Edward Arnold.

BBC News (2016) Sir Philip Green left BHS on 'life support', MPs find. [online] Available at: www.bbc.co.uk/news/business-36879241 (accessed 23 March 2017).

Blandin, J and Machin, S (2007) *Recent Changes in Intergenerational Mobility in Britain*. London: Sutton Trust. [online] Available at: http://cep.lse.ac.uk/pubs/download/special/Recent_Changes_in_Intergenerational_Mobility_in_Britain.pdf (accessed 23 March 2017).

The Equality Trust [online] Available at: www.equalitytrust.org.uk (accessed 23 March 2017).

Ferguson, I and Woodward, R (2009) *Radical Social Work in Practice*. Bristol: Policy Press.

Lavalette, M (ed) (2011) *Radical Social Work Today*. Bristol: Policy Press.

Social Work Action Network (SWAN) [online] Available at: www.socialworkfuture.org (accessed 23 March 2017).

Stacey, K (2014) The real story of the miners' strike in five questions [blog], 3 January. [online] Available at: http://blogs.ft.com/westminster/2014/01/the-real-story-of-the-miners-strike-in-five-questions/ (accessed 23 March 2017).

The Sutton Trust [online] Available at: www.suttontrust.com (accessed 23 March 2017).

Turbett, C (2014) *Doing Radical Social Work*. Basingstoke: Palgrave Macmillan.

Worthington, D (2014) Looking back on the three day week. London: New Historian. [online] Available at: www.newhistorian.com/looking-back-three-day-week/2405/ (accessed 23 March 2017).

Articles from the *Journal of Critical and Radical Social Work*

Chapter 3 | Theoretically driven approaches to social work intervention

An important distinction is made between the content of Chapter 2 and Chapter 3. Chapter 2 considered four theories which offer an explanation for why people behave the way they do. This chapter will consider four different approaches to social work intervention which although are underpinned by a theoretical construction, do not offer an explanation for why people behave the way they do. Nevertheless, they offer a distinctive method of intervention that corresponds to their associated theoretical construction.

The four approaches are:

strengths-based approaches;

existential approaches;

humanistic approaches;

problem-solving approaches.

The approach under consideration will be applied to the case study we have been working with in Chapter 2.

LEARNING OUTCOMES

By the end of this chapter you should understand the rudiments of and see how strengths-based approaches, existential approaches, humanistic approaches and problem-solving approaches can be applied to a case study.

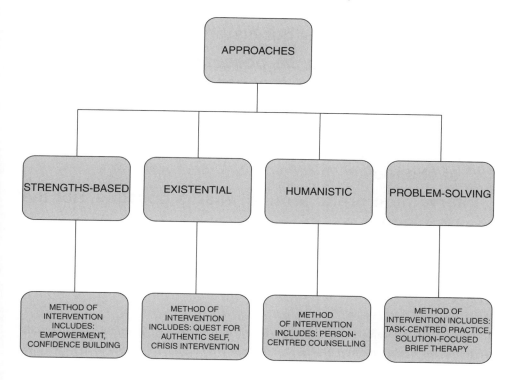

STRENGTHS-BASED APPROACHES

Headlines

Yes we can!

We are not bound by our histories and traditions.

Even in hard times we possess inner resourceful-ness and resilience that can be drawn on, encour-aged and engaged to enable us to cope, survive and achieve.

We are capable; we are capable of growth, capable of change.

Intervention orbits around what is possible, not the problems.

Introduction to strengths-based approaches

A principal proponent of the strengths-based approach is D Saleebey, an American academic, formerly a mental health practitioner who defined the approach as follows. The formula of the strengths-based approach is simple:

Rally clients' interests, capacities, motivations, resources and emotions in the work of reaching their hopes and dreams, help them find pathways to those goals and the payoff may be an enhanced quality of daily life for them.

(Saleebey, 2009, p 1)

Let's try a thought experiment; what words do you associate with someone who says they have a life coach? Make a note of them. Now do the same exercise again but this time the person says they have a social worker. Now compare the two lists. At the risk of exposing our prejudices, I suspect the list in response to the person with the life coach conjures up a more positive image. Well, while the social worker cannot simply describe themselves as a life coach, they can, in adopting a strengths-based approach, bring a more optimistic air to their involvement by emphasising what can be achieved rather than what's going wrong. In this respect, the strengths-based approach can be described as an empowerment model of intervention. A strengths-based approach steers well clear of reconstructing the stigma-bearing 'deficit' or 'flawed' view of a service user's functioning and seeks to shrink the potential for 'problems' to dominate the professional relationship.

Karen Healey, in her book, *Social Work Theories in Context*, draws on the work of Saleebey and Weick et al in identifying a list of what she describes as practice assumptions applicable to a strengths-based approach which include:

> » All people have strengths, capacities and resources.
>
> » People usually demonstrate resilience, rather than pathology in the face of adverse life events.
>
> » Service users have the capacity to determine what is best for them.
>
> » The focus of strengths-based work is on the service users' capacities and those of their communities.
>
> » Collaborative partnerships between workers and service users reflect and help build these capacities.

She goes on to develop five principles for practice:

> » Adopt a hopeful, optimistic attitude.
>
> » Focus primarily on assets.
>
> » Collaborate with the service user.
>
> » Work toward the long-term empowerment.
>
> » Create community.

(Healy, 2014, pp 168–72)

The theoretical underpinning for the strengths-based approach is derived from questioning what can be achieved from a climate of implied criticism, given the impact that negative stereotyping and labelling can have on one's self-esteem; and recognition of the role resilience can play if mobilised in the service of self-efficacy.

A strengths-based approach would firstly recognise and accentuate what is working well. Secondly, there would be a recognition of the skills, commitment and endeavour that have gone into achieving 'what works well'. Difficult times, even if they are current, can be set in the context of *despite x and y the person is still managing to maintain what is working well*. It may be acknowledged that going through bad times is common to most people's lives and despite the tendency to feel 'alone' with one's troubles, they are unlikely to be unique to the person concerned. It may be useful to explore the bad times previously endured. This would create the opportunity to point out that such times *have* been endured before and to recognise the resilience and emotional durability the person must have been able to draw on to have survived and continued with their lives. For example, an approved mental health practitioner (AMHP) working with a recently diagnosed bipolar service user may enquire as to how they feel having the diagnosis and a *label*; acknowledge that symptoms will not have only recently appeared; therefore, the service user will have been managing their condition for some time and are likely to be very knowledgeable about how the condition manifests and how best to manage it. The AMHP might allude to the episodic nature of the condition and enquire as to the proportion of time when the service user's function is significantly impaired (likely to be less than the majority). The AMHP may ask about what strategies the service user puts in place to cope at such times but also enquire as to what the service user achieves when function is not impaired or during more industrious periods when function may be enhanced.

A strengths-based approach is theoretically boundless. It could encompass further developments with our bipolar service user who shows insight into how they manage the condition and what services they find most helpful. This is both recognised and encouraged by the AMHP, who, through a research interest is writing a paper on the condition for a conference. The service user contributes to the paper, which leads to a co-presentation of the paper. This exposure leads to the service user being invited to take part in a national steering group to help develop and shape the provision of services for this user group. Such developments towards collaborative partnerships may require intermediate steps such as training in presentation skills, for example, but the emphasis is on working towards ever-increasing equality within the relationship between the practitioner and service user and the avoidance of patronage or tokenism.

Critical readers may think this example is a little far-fetched but a social worker embracing a strengths-based approach would say '*Why not?*' and counter the charge of being fanciful with the idea that the greatest limiting factor as to what can be achieved is ourselves.

A social worker using this approach would also want to explore what their service user identified as not working well and would want them to describe what would be different if it was how they wanted it to be. This would scope the desired change necessary and indicate if this was realistic and achievable. If not, a compromise may be considered which could still represent positive change.

The use of language

The strengths-based approach demonstrates and utilises the important role the language we use has in constructing the image, meaning and conveying value to what is being described. The Paralympic Games have introduced a new image of people with disabilities from that of people managing their disability to that of athletic endeavour, striving to achieve and become medal winners. Other examples include describing people who have experienced abuse as *survivors* rather than *victims*, and within mental health services using the term *recovery teams* rather than the focus being on acute illness. This is more than being obliging to notions of 'political correctness'. The language we use constructs our world. Some words confer value; consider the word *scrounger* often used in the popular press and compare this with the 'value-neutral' alternative, *person who is eligible to claim welfare benefit*. When the Spastics Society changed its name to Scope, the term of abuse so often used in playground scuffles began to be eradicated.

The language provided by the medical model, characterised by objective and abstract terms, may provide a succinct diagnosis but does little to convey the human face of the person being described.

For example, a young person with cerebral palsy could be described like this:

- » Hemiplegic.
- » Poor gait.
- » Dysgraphia.
- » Hyper-verbal.

Or like this:

- » Enjoys strong family support.
- » Walks unaided despite limp.
- » Writes fluently with computer assistance.
- » Extroverted.
- » Confident.

(Adapted from Parrish, 2014, p 261)

The need to exercise sensitivity, care and consideration in the language we use is a requirement in any caring profession such as social work and is not the preserve of a strengths-based approach. However, this approach does invite the social worker to consider the opportunities to *reframe* a problem, to accentuate the positive and in doing so create a platform upon which to build with an optimistic orientation. For example, a school pupil whose attendance is poor, regularly being absent for two days per week does in fact attend for three days! Recognition of the pupil's ability, skills and talents that enable this can be built upon to promote achieving full attendance.

The importance of language was emphasised by Saleebey himself, who said its power could be used to '*elevate and inspire or demoralise and destroy*' (Saleebey, 2012, p 11).

The service user's narratives and expertise

Saleebey asserts that '*in order to detect a service user's strengths the social worker must be genuinely interested in and respectful of their stories, narratives and accounts – the interpretive angles they take on their own experiences*' (Saleebey, 2012, p 15). David Howe, in his book *A Brief Introduction to Social Work Theory*, suggests that '*service users have a surprising amount of knowledge and expertise about their lives, their relationships and how to survive*' (Howe, 2009, p 102). Such ideas have developed into the notion of the service user as expert, and applied as narrative theory and therapy. A fundamental element of any intervention of a practitioner from a caring profession is gathering an understanding of their service user's thoughts and feelings and a sense of their reality. To suggest that they should be anything other than interested and respectful of these would be perverse. However, the service user's perspective is central in a strengths-based approach, as this contains not only the ingredients that have brought the service user to where they are but also the seeds of progress to enable them to move forward. The role of the practitioner is to nurture the growth of those seeds.

The application of a strengths-based approach to social work practice

It may be apparent that the application of a strengths-based approach is ideally suited to intervention where the social worker has the role of being an advocate for their primary service user. For example, assisting a young person with disabilities achieve their goal of living independently. Nevertheless, it may be applied to good effect in most social work practice settings, although the extent may vary in accordance with what is appropriate. For example, a young offender may have many qualities but their prowess in motor vehicle theft cannot be celebrated. Working with involuntary service users does not, of itself, preclude applying a strengths-based approach but for reasons that will become apparent its efficacy may be limited where intervention conveys some degree of social censure, intended or otherwise, as in child protection work. In such cases it may be worth considering who might be best placed to apply a predominantly strengths-based approach. For example, in a co-worked case a Home-Start volunteer could work with a parent as their *primary service user* and fully utilise a strengths-based approach whereas the children and families' social worker has to maintain the focus on the welfare of the child, even where the majority, if not all the 'work' is undertaken with the caregivers.

Many social workers would say they apply a strengths-based approach as they do seek opportunities to accentuate the positives where they can. However, this approach, if applied as its proponents intended, is much more than donning an optimistic attitude. I do not intend to discount this, or detract from its impact. Indeed, a common goal of any social work intervention is to enable the service user to feel better about themselves, as a child or young person, a woman or a man, a caregiver, a person, and the result of so doing can be enduring and the pinnacle of some intervention. But a full-blown application of the approach would aim to extend the concept of partnership working to that of equality in the relationship and co-membership of communities, which would be beyond the reach for some statutory social work intervention and its appropriateness questionable. A compromise may be achieved through the implementation of a framework for practice that uses a strengths-based orientation such as Triple P or Signs of Safety. These frameworks are designed to be applied to working with families to address concerns for the welfare of children. The outcome of such intervention must include the potential for a child's removal where they cannot be safeguarded at home but this does not rule out commencing any intervention with the positive orientation of the strengths-based approach. Triple P (Positive Parenting Program) is designed to help caregivers foster and promote positive, healthy relationships between them and the children in their care. Signs of Safety is an alternative framework with similar aims and offers a structured, uniform approach to working with children and families. The framework was devised by Turnell and Edwards in the late 1990s in Western Australia and offers the practitioner a systemised method for undertaking assessment, direct work and evaluation. Naming the programme Signs of Safety gives an unmistakable nod to a strengths-based approach but the system does include a *danger statement* in which concerns for the welfare of the child(ren) are clearly set out. The system helpfully employs a scaling tool which is designed to compare the concerns the practitioners have with those of the caregivers. Many local authorities in England have adopted these programmes, training their staff and embedding the system in their organisations.

Let's see how a strengths-based approach could be applied to our case study. We are using the same case study, the basic details of which remain largely unchanged. This time however, the case material is presented as a snapshot of how firstly, Annette, and secondly, the social worker, are feeling today to illustrate how this approach may be applied and its challenges to *accentuate the positives* when confronting the realities in people's lives. This *snapshot of thoughts* is taken just before the social worker is due to visit Annette, Ben and Sam.

Case study

Annette

You are feeling down in the dumps today. Andy is off the scene at present, and you are partly relieved but miss adult company. You do not miss his verbal and physical abuse but you wonder if that is all you are going to get in life. There is not much you can think of that you can describe as good things that have happened in your life: you were neglected and on the child protection register as a child; you were pregnant when you were a teenager, now have two kids and have little support from their fathers; both kids are subject to children-in-need plans; you are in social housing on a rundown estate in an economically depressed area; you currently take a size 18 and feel Andy's taunts of being 'a fat slob' are true rather than abusive. You are the young, one-parent family on benefits that the papers go on about as 'scroungers'. There is no one that you feel you can call on who can offer you reliable support. Kids come round mainly for somewhere to hang out rather than seek your company. You don't see much that you have to smile about and cannot see things changing but you quite like chatting to the social worker who despite all that, seems interested in you.

The social worker

You are really feeling positive and optimistic about your work with Annette. You are seeing an improved level of physical interaction between her and her children. You might not say as much but you regard the fact that Andy is currently off the scene as a positive development as you are sure Annette could find a more suitable and supportive partner. You are becoming increasingly impressed with some of Annette's qualities and personal attributes, her resilience for example at surviving such a difficult childhood. You know she does not have the support of parents but you are aware they did little to meet her needs when they had the opportunity, quite the opposite in fact, so she might be better off emotionally investing in other relationships/friendships, perhaps with women in similar situations to herself. You know that she enjoyed working in the retail trade and felt she made a positive contribution then, but she continues to do now providing for and 'being there' for her two healthy, beautiful children. When they are a little older she could look for work.

You believe she has a high level of personal resourcefulness and you are confident in your ability to enable Annette to recognise this. She is a householder in her own right, does not have rent arrears and is beginning to take control of who enters her home. You can help reframe a number of characteristics that she tends to see as negative in her life: she is a survivor rather than victim. OK, she is not happy being a size 18 but the woman's average in the UK is 16 so there is not much to do there. She was good at sport and reading and could be more of a role model to children, only allowing the occasional visit outside school hours. The average age of single parents is in the thirties, whereas she will still be young when her kids are grown up and will be able to enjoy her grandchildren. Claiming benefits as a main source of income can make people feel bad, in terms of self-respect and self-esteem, not helped by some papers describing them as scroungers but the claimant may see themselves as exercising their right to claim the appropriate benefit. You are interested in how things will work out as you feel Annette has inner strength to help her overcome adversity. You feel you would like to spend more time having a chat and investing a bit more time and energy to assist and witness the change you are sure Annette has the ability to bring about rather than 'monitor' her as a service user. On your impending visit you intend to list all the things Annette does for the children that are successful at meeting their needs, in so doing demonstrating to Annette that she is capable of providing good enough parenting despite the lack of good role models.

On the visit the social worker avoids making reference to any deficiencies in the quality of care Annette provides for the children. On the contrary, the social worker identifies what Annette does for Ben and Sam that works well and meets their needs and praises her for her abilities and efforts. The social worker picks up on Annette's mood and gently parries this with some of her own thoughts as illustrated. She may want to explore an achievable objective Annette identifies for herself as something desired and would have the effect of improving something in her situation. In discussing such an objective, a pathway towards its realisation may emerge.

The circumstances of the social worker's involvement, that of concern for the welfare of Ben and Sam, precludes the departure from conventional social work practice envisaged by Saleebey's application of a purely strengths-based approach (Saleebey,

2002, p1). However, those circumstances include multiple opportunities to accentuate the positives, mobilise Annette's capacity and self-efficacy and help build confidence.

Application of the frameworks briefly identified as Triple P and Signs of Safety would also be appropriate but specific training for practitioners is required.

Some personal reflections on intervention drawing on the ideas of a strengths-based approach.

The effective application of this approach is a skilled, creative undertaking. As illustrated in the case study, the terrain that a strengths-based orientation brings could be quite alien to a service user and may not resonate with their experience. It is important that its application is pitched in a manner that is authentic and genuine. It may be necessary to balance what is possible with what the service user can recognise. In order to gain the perspective a balloon flight offers, it is first necessary to gradually inflate the canopy while tethered to the ground.

In Chapter 1, 'Setting the scene', consideration was given to the role of the social worker according to the circumstances through which social work engagement occurs. The continuum may be represented like this:

by Statute ——— by coercion ——— by invitation or request ——— community development
⟶

While a strengths-based approach could be employed, to some degree, in all these circumstances, it is my view that the extent to which it could authentically be the dominant method of intervention increases in the direction of travel of the arrow.

As the nature of involvement with Annette is somewhere around the *by coercion* area of the continuum, opportunities to apply a strengths-based approach should be sought where possible but it is unrealistic to suggest it could be the sole approach taken to the exclusion of all the other methods of intervention considered in this book. One of the reasons why this is the case is related to the nature of the referral that instigated social work involvement. There is no getting away from the implication that there exists some shortfall between the quality of child-rearing practices Annette is currently giving Sam and Ben and those that would be sufficient to meet their perceived needs. Indeed, where this is not the case, imposing social work intervention would be inappropriate and oppressive. Contained within the shortfall is some lack of provision, either through acts of omission (she does not know how to better meet their needs) or commission (she is unwilling to better meet their needs) and should be directly addressed. While the social worker could and *should* recognise Annette's knowledge of her own history, the validity of her hopes and desires, assumptions cannot be made as to the insight she has gained through her experiences as this needs to be assessed. Nor could she be currently considered an *expert* in executing child-rearing practices. Society, through the organs of the state, is saying that the child-rearing practices Sam and Ben are currently subject to require the expertise of the social worker to facilitate an improvement in these.

Contrast this with social work intervention that has come about through a wheelchair user's request to have their dwelling adapted through the provision of a ramp, and some modifications to the kitchen. Here the service user is likely to have a very good understanding of what they need to gain access and better utilise their kitchen and may legitimately claim being 'expert' in knowing their needs. Hence, the extent to which the service user can be considered 'expert' in the objective sense is dependent on the context. However, this should not detract from seeking to maximise the extent to which the service user may be considered 'expert' in whatever element is being considered as this is the hallmark of the strengths-based approach.

References and further reading

Healy, K (2005) *Social Work Theories in Context*. Basingstoke: Palgrave Macmillan.

Healy, K (2014) *Social Work Theories in Context Creating Frameworks for Practice*. Basingstoke: Palgrave Macmillan.

Howe, D (2009) *A Brief Introduction to Social Work Theory*. Basingstoke: Palgrave Macmillan.

Parrish, M (2014) *Social Work Perspectives on Human Behaviour*. Maidenhead: Open University Press.

Saleebey, D (2002) Introduction: Power in the People, in Saleebey, D (ed) *The Strengths Perspective in Social Work Practice* (3rd ed). Boston: Allyn and Bacon, pp 1–22.

Saleebey, D (2009) *Strengths Perspective in Social Work* (5th ed). Boston: Pearson.

Saleebey, D (2012) *The Strengths Perspective in Social Work Practice* (6th ed). Cambridge: Pearson.

Turnell, A and Edwards, S (1997) Aspiring to Partnership: The Signs of Safety Approach to Child Protection. *Child Abuse Review*, 6(3): 179–90.

Turnell, A and Murphy, T (2014) *Signs of Safety Comprehensive Briefing Paper* (3rd ed). Perth, Australia: Resolutions Consultancy Pty Ltd.

EXISTENTIAL APPROACHES

Headlines

Man is nothing else but what he makes of himself (Sartre, 2002).

Our existence is bound within the 'knowable' world.

One's existence is a 'no frills', one-way flight in a universe indifferent to it.

Associated with humanism.

Free will is important. Individuals are free to make choices, to choose courses of action (they cannot do anything other than this).

To act is to make a choice. We and we alone are responsible for these freely chosen actions.

We remake our ethics every time we choose a course of action.

Introduction to existential approaches

In order to appreciate what an existential approach to social work might look like, we first need a basic understanding of existentialism.

Existentialism is a philosophical perspective most closely associated with the work of Jean Paul Sartre (1905–1980), the French intellectual and philosopher. It is concerned with ontology, the study of being. It invites us to face up to the big questions about the nature and purpose of existence, which can make us feel uncomfortable, insecure and which some of us may prefer to avoid. **Authenticity** is the acceptance of choice and responsibility for our actions. **Bad faith** is where avoidance of facing this leads to the denial of authenticity – considered to be a lie to oneself. Sartre said that we are '*condemned to be free*', which implies, at best, something unpleasant. This can be understood once the consequence of being authentic is realised. Authenticity confers the *weight* of responsibility for oneself, one's choices and actions to the exclusion of anything else such as our personality, partners, parents, God, fate or destiny to share or take responsibility. As soon as one is autonomous, in that one has the capacity to make conscious decisions, then one is not only free to make them but doing so is an inescapable consequence of being. There may be ancillary factors such as dependents to consider but this does not dilute the central tenant of ownership of the choices made. For example, a family argument is under way, the truculent teenager is berating their parent for their shortfalls in failing to provide x, y and z. The parent, in defence, lists what they have done for the teenager, citing a, b and c and the sacrifices they have made for them. We may even be familiar with such a scenario, but we can see why this strategy is unlikely to quell the teenager's dissatisfaction as the parent is trying to make the child responsible for their decisions, firstly of having the child and secondly providing him or her with a, b and c, for if that was indeed at the parent's personal cost then they made that choice, or so the existentialist and perhaps the teenager would argue.

In existentialism there is no intrinsic meaning to existence. Whatever meaning is ascribed to existence is derived from the experience of living that existence. This unadorned view of the nature of existence can seem bleak and perhaps is, as the comfort blanket of even imagining some cosmic source of beneficence is somehow looking out for you is not available. In this way existentialism is atheistic. This does not of course detract from the benefits of supportive, loving interpersonal relationships, or the human capacity to find beauty in nature. However, for the existentialist, *existence* comes before *essence*. So God could not have had the idea: '*I'm a bit lonely, I will create man*' and then man existed. Equally *human nature* could not come before man's existence. In fact, an existentialist would not countenance that humans have a *nature* common to them. What, for example, is common to the ways in which Hitler and Gandhi chose to act? We will leave these more esoteric ideas to the philosophers.

The quest for the authentic self

A practical application of existentialism may be the quest of an existentialist to become and present themselves in as true an expression of themselves as possible, to be authentic to themselves. For example, the person who chooses a distinctive hairstyle, hair colour or clothing may be doing so as an expression of their true selves or simply going along with what is currently fashionable. Only the former is pertinent to the existentialist.

So, first we exist and then begin the task of becoming the person we would recognise as us. The sentient person forges who they are, adopting values, views and ways of living to come to a point where they can say, '*This is me!*' This second period of gestation may be turbulent or have turbulent periods. Adolescence and what is loosely termed *mid-life* are stages in the life course associated with turbulence; the former confronts questions such as: '*Who am I?*' And the latter: '*What should I do with what remains of my life?*' It has been suggested that the expression on the face of the person in Edvard Munch's painting, *The Scream* (1893), represents the existential angst when one's true place in the universe is realised. However, provided a reasonable standard of mental health is achieved, these times of turbulence and angst are transitory and do not feature so as to significantly perturb one's sense of self. So we gather around ourselves the abilities and skills, people and pets, habits and interests, occupations and lifestyles that we associate with ourselves, the things that make us who we are. We appear to settle into the comfort and security this *homeostasis* or steady-state provides. However, events, even those anticipated and welcomed, can disrupt it and present a need to reconfigure our perception of *who we are* in order to adjust to and accommodate these events.

'*Events, dear boy, events...*'

This was the answer the Prime Minister Harold Macmillan was said to have replied when a journalist asked him what was most likely to blow his government off course. (Harris, 2002) A government is subject to world events but even those that occur in one's life may be disruptive:

Life course events (anticipated)	Life change events (unanticipated)
Adolescence and independence	Injury resulting in disability
Marriage or partnership	Divorce or separation
Parenthood	Serious illness
Death of parent	Death of spouse or child
Retirement	Redundancy

This is far from an exhaustive list of events that can present a threat to one's homeostasis and confront us with the need to adjust to and accommodate change. There is no intention to prescribe a qualitative difference between what may be described as *anticipated* as opposed to *unanticipated* events as how they are reacted to will depend on individual circumstances. The death of a pet or a grandparent can be acutely disruptive to our sense of self even where they are anticipated. Gilliland and James cite the term '*developmental crises*' for events associated with the life course and '*situational crises*' to unforeseen events. (Gilliland and James, 1997, p 19).

A developmental crisis may require the person concerned to come to terms with and adjust to the lifestyle the *changed state* imposes. A situational crisis, such as having witnessed or been caught up in a train crash or terrorist atrocity, may require the person concerned to have the opportunity to talk about their traumatic event, as if the re-telling enables acceptance. However, where they suffered severe injuries such as the loss of a limb they may need to grieve the loss of their former self and become acquainted with and accept the 'new' version of themselves.

It is events that 'come out of the blue' and have life-changing consequences that are characterised as having the capacity to be the most traumatic and can result in an *existential crisis* – literally a crisis in and to our very existence and what we think *is* our existence. Surviving an existential crisis requires resources and a level of resilience greater than what we usually draw on as coping mechanisms, resulting in a lack of knowledge or experience of how to navigate the devastated terrain we find ourselves in. Sometimes these hitherto unplumbed resources, resilience and knowledge are beyond our grasp and the ultimate decision is made not to continue with our lives. The tragic events which befell PC Rathbone serves as a reminder as to the potential fragility of our notion of homeostasis. Constable Rathbone was sat in his police car when he was shot and blinded by lone gunman Raoul Moat in 2010. This event started several others which included the permanent loss of his sight, the loss of his job, the end of his marriage and ultimately that of his life.

The application of existential approaches to social work practice

The reader will find more comprehensive and complex analyses of the application of existentialism to social work through further reading. Neil Thompson's book, *Existentialism and Social Work*, will prove a very good source. For the purposes of this book, two applications of existential approaches to social work are identified. The first is described as promoting autonomy and the second as crisis intervention. Readers of other books on social work theory may find *crisis intervention* grouped with other *problem-solving* approaches. This does not make either author 'wrong' as such. I have included it here through its association as a method of intervention in existential crises.

Promoting autonomy

Many social workers can doubtless recall situations in which they have worked to support the service user make changes that really hold the prospect for betterment in their lives and those of their dependants, but the invitation has not been taken up. There may be several reasons for this. For example, engaging in change is threatening and many people find it hard to do; the social worker is being paternalistic and is not taking account of what the service user wants, to name but two. Whatever the reason, this outcome is entirely justified if the service user has capacity to come to a determination that they are living as they wish and providing this is not harming themselves or others they are responsible for, so be it and the services withdraw. But *have* they come to such a determination? If they say as much then it may be assumed they have but what if they are in a routine, a rut, re-living their family's habits in a way that cannot be described as a positive choice but just *going through the motions*? In this situation the basic idea of existentialism may have something to say that could stimulate change.

For example, Mike is 52. He was made redundant when he was 48 and his life took a downturn at this time and he separated from his partner. He now lives alone in a mobile home on a caravan park in the suburbs of a rural town. He is unemployed, suffers with depression and drinks alcohol on a daily basis. His routine rarely changes, visiting his 'local' at lunch times and evening. The pub has a dowdy, run-down appearance and has few customers, especially in the weekdays. Mike usually relies on takeaway food for his evening meal. He buys a daily newspaper from the local newsagent and does a weekly shop at the supermarket. Apart from these outings he rarely goes out/elsewhere and spends time watching daytime TV.

Mike's support worker has got to know him a little over the course of her visits. She thinks of him as an affable man but he lost some of his 'get up and go' when he was made redundant. Mike appears to see the resulting downturn in the quality of his life as an inevitable consequence of losing his job which was important to him. The support worker is aware of the existential approach and gently challenges Mike about the lifestyle choices he is making, linking these to the way in which they contribute to his depression. Mike initially denied he was *choosing* to go to the pub, watching daytime TV and buying takeaway food but the practitioner persisted that this was in fact the case. She took the line that these choices were '*his to make*' provided he took responsibility for the consequences of those choices. Mike was defensive, suggesting that the boredom, loneliness and depression left him no choice but to do what he did and felt they were linked as if in a loop. He implied he was the victim of that loop, appearing to be incapable of entertaining the idea that he might be its orchestrator. The practitioner suggested he thinks about how he might break this 'loop' and explored with him alternative choices as to how he occupied his time. This included going up into the town, going for a coffee in one of those places that have lounge seats and books, visiting a wine bar or different pubs with different and livelier clientele, shopping in the market, planning a menu, selecting foodstuffs and cooking for himself. In this way the practitioner can promote the autonomy of the service user and responsibility for the choices made.

Crisis intervention

The experience of facing a crisis such as that resulting from the events listed in the table on page 96 is common to many if not most of us at some point or another in our lives. If we are fairly robust, can call on good social capital through family and friends, possess inner resourcefulness and resilience and the event represents one crisis rather than several, we may come through without the need for professional intervention. However, where our circumstances and characteristics are different, increasing our vulnerability, or the crisis represents one of existential proportions, intervention may be required.

It would be unwise to try to be more prescriptive. Accurately anticipating how someone will cope or is coping with a crisis is problematic. Many people experience separation and divorce and the emotional upset it brings can be deeply distressing, especially for the respondent. It usually represents a crisis for the couple concerned, any children they have and on occasion members of the extended family, especially where ensuing arrangements for children result in loss of contact. Separation and divorce can represent an existential crisis for some who cannot envisage living with this status or is unaccepting of it. Such people may never *move on*. Moreover, for a few, despite outwardly appearing to have much to live for, not only take their own lives but tragically those of their family too. Suicidal or homicidal ideation does not have to be present for a crisis to have existential proportions but representing a challenge to the person's sense of existence and what they would recognise as constituting them. One might think the incidence of people experiencing existential crises is relatively rare but a delay in recognition, resulting in post-traumatic stress disorder and the fact that suicide is the biggest cause of death in males aged 20–34 in the UK (Office of National Statistics, cited in Davies, 2015), would suggest it is not as rare as one might think.

The aim of intervening in a crisis at its most basic is to 'be there', in so doing providing a 'handrail' for the person undergoing the crisis to grab. This handrail itself may not feel solid, as it is metaphorically attached to the same storm-drenched deck, but it can represent something to hang on to while the pitching and rolling of *self* is at its worst. Thankfully this intense period is time-limited, the pitching and rolling subsides and some semblance of equilibrium emerges. Experiencing the *crisis* stage of a trauma is considered to be, for most, around six to eight weeks in duration. Accordingly, *crisis intervention* is a short-term initiative. This does not mean that one is usually 'over' the trauma in such a timeframe as psychological upheavals of these dimensions can result in a variety of outcomes, from that of leaving residual issues such as depression to that of a healthy *growing through and out of* the experience. The presence and quality of support in the immediate aftermath of the crisis will influence the outcome.

Models of crisis intervention

Burl Gilliland and Richard James, in their book *Crisis Intervention Strategies*, cite the work of Leitner and Belkin in identifying three models of crisis intervention. These are the equilibrium model, the cognitive model and the psycho-social transition model. The equilibrium model seeks to address the early phase of crisis by introducing some element of stabilising the degree of disorientation. The cognitive model seeks to address 'faulty thinking' such as in the case of denying one's responsibility for the choices made, as illustrated in the example of *Mike*. There are parallels to Beck's work on CBT with the cognitive model, discussed in Chapter 2. The psycho-social transition model is linked to transitions through the life course and has parallels with Erikson's developmental stages that we also considered in Chapter 2.

Gilliland developed a generic *six-step model* of intervention in crises (Gilliland and James, 1997, p 28). The first three steps are concerned with *listening*:

1. To how the service user describes their crisis (*define the problem).*

2. To any threats or dangers to the service user's safety (*ensure client safety*).

3. Demonstrate attentive interpersonal skills (*provide support).*

The second three steps are concerned with *action:*

4. Explore choices and options (*examine alternatives).*

5. Decide on 'things to do' (*make plans).*

6. Ownership of plan (*obtain commitment).*

Let's consider how an existential approach might be applied to the case study we are working with.

Case study

Used to promote autonomy

The presenting circumstances have not changed. Annette's two children are considered 'children in need' due to concerns for some aspects of the quality of care and supervision they receive. From having read the case notes, the social worker knows that Annette's name was on the child protection register when she was a child, under the category of neglect, but Annette confirmed this herself when the social worker took a personal history. The social worker would be interested in any comparisons between the care she received and that which she provides for Ben and Sam and could gently enquire about Annette's view on this. Assuming some comparison could be drawn, the social worker would ask Annette why she thought this was? If Annette implied in her response that some form of repetition was occurring, the social worker might then ask Annette how this might be working. There are some options here but the line of enquiry is very useful for assessment purposes as Annette's answers may reveal the degree of insight she has into her own needs and those of her children. If she said she had no role models to learn from, there may be acts of omission and introducing Annette to parenting classes may be appropriate. If she said she copied what she experienced, social learning theory may explain what's going on but if she gave the impression she thought it was inevitable and did not 'own' whole or partial responsibility then an existential approach could be used to encourage her to see that she is choosing the 'open door', choosing to allow the supervision of the children to be undertaken by strangers, choosing to neglect the house and not to dispose of the dirty nappies. Through such challenge the social worker can promote Annette's sense of autonomy and responsibility.

Used in crisis intervention

Firstly an update on the circumstances.

Over the past six weeks Andy has been spending more time with Annette. They see they have really no one else apart from each other and the children. They have decided to try to make a go of it. Andy has moved in and is taking part in a methadone programme. He is supporting Annette with childcare and the couple are feeling positive about the future.

Today the social worker arrived at their office to find a message from the emergency duty team who had attended Annette's address at 4am that morning. Annette had been described as hysterical by a paramedic who had attended in response to her 999 call after she'd tried to revive Andy, who was unconscious after using heroin. The paramedics declared him dead at the scene. A post-mortem would go on to confirm what was suspected, that Andy had died of an overdose. A sample of what he had used was analysed and found to be of exceptional strength. This would have had an even greater impact as he had not used since being on the methadone programme, which had weakened his tolerance to the opiate. Annette had not been aware of his relapse.

The social worker visited Annette to find her distraught. It wasn't just Andy's death, though it was a huge shock, but just when they had a chance, it had been snatched away, she sobbed. In an understandable confused mix of emotions she expressed anger at Andy and blamed him for relapsing, then felt guilty for wanting him to go on the methadone programme. She described how she'd tried to revive him and then just seemed numb as if in shock. The social worker asked if she could put the kettle on.

If the social worker applied Gilliland's six steps:

The social worker just listens to Annette talk through the jumbled range of thoughts and emotions, and just 'goes with' what she expresses.

» The social worker listens for anything that may indicate Annette is thinking or feeling like harming herself or harbouring any other self-destructive urges.

» The social worker concentrates on what Annette is saying, demonstrating skills in active listening and attending, using minimal encouragers such as nodding, occasionally paraphrasing but is OK with silences too, not needing to 'fill the gaps'.

» The social worker enquires of Annette if there are things she feels she needs to do, and if there is anything she would like her to do, including help with childcare. (The social worker could arrange for some short-term nursery care if that was appropriate; alternatively, Annette may feel she needs her children close to her and the social worker could arrange for a family support worker to offer some short-term care in the home.)

» The social worker and Annette make a list of things to do. This includes telling the children and Andy's estranged sister; establishing next of kin and if there was no one else, registering the death; sorting through his things; thinking about the funeral arrangements – the social worker would look into costs and the local authority's contribution where there are insufficient funds.

» The social worker raises the issue of whether or not Annette thinks that some bereavement counselling through Cruse would help. Annette is unsure but agrees to try it. The social worker says she will make arrangements and says she will visit Annette weekly for the next six weeks.

Hopefully, these brief illustrations show how the social worker may intervene in the crisis that has befallen Annette, constructing a 'handrail' which she can cling onto while she adjusts to the new terrain of life without Andy.

Some personal reflections on intervention drawing on the ideas of existential approaches to social work practice

Existentialism holds that people create their destiny through the choices they make as they live their lives, and could not accept the suggestion that one's destiny is somehow preordained and all one can do is to live the life 'set out' for you. Such a notion minimises one's autonomy and anyone subscribing to this notion would be exhibiting bad faith by denying their capacity for authenticity. It follows that anyone adopting a belief system which limits or denies their autonomy and freedom to act authentically also attract the charge of bad faith. However, would it be reasonable to level this charge at someone whose religious faith obliges them to put their trust in their God for their actions and the direction their life takes? Rationally the answer must be yes but would this be ethical social work practice? How might the practitioner adopting an existentialist approach show respect for someone's religious faith? The same problem occurs with certain cultural practices. It is easier and of course, necessary, to oppose these where they result in child abuse such as in alleged demonic possession (as in the cases of Victoria Climbié and Khyra Ishaq) and the practice of female genital mutilation. It is however more difficult and perhaps inappropriate to apply an existential approach with service users who hold strong religious convictions or beliefs in fate and destiny. For example, I recall a couple who described themselves as Hindu. They explained the birth of their severely disabled child as being due to an unspecified (wrongful) act by the female, in a former life. There are several problems with this from a human-rights perspective but the saddest consequence was that for the mother, her child was a manifestation of guilt. However, as Hinduism appeared so central to their identity I did not challenge the thinking but restricted my involvement to care planning. Such reservations may not prevent a practitioner from acquainting the service user with the perspective offered through an existential approach, provided that this was presented as an option although the approach is likely to have limited potency. However, with strict religious devotees such ideas could be considered heretical and cause offence.

References and further reading

BBC News (2012) Raoul Moat victim PC David Rathband found dead at home. [online] Available at: www.bbc.co.uk/news/uk-england-tyne-17216389 (accessed 24 March 2017).

Davies, C (2015) Number of suicides in UK increases, with male rate highest since 2001. *The Guardian*, 19 February. [online] Available at: www.theguardian.com/society/2015/feb/19/number-of-suicides-uk-increases-2013-male-rate-highest-2001 (accessed 24 March 2017).

Gilliland, B and James, R (1997) *Crisis Intervention Strategies*. London: Thomson.

Harris, R (2002) As Macmillan never said: that's enough quotations. *The Telegraph*, 4 June. [online] Available at: www.telegraph.co.uk/comment/personal-view/3577416/As-Macmillan-never-said-thats-enough-quotations.html (accessed 24 March 2017).

Munch, E (1893) *The Scream*. Oslo, Norway: Eduard Munch.org. [online] Available at: www.edvardmunch.org/the-scream.jsp (accessed 24 March 2017).

Parrish, M (2010) *Social Work Perspectives on Human Behaviour*. Maidenhead: Open University Press.

Payne, M (2005) *Modern Social Work Theory*. Basingstoke: Palgrave Macmillan.

Sartre, J P (2002) *Existentialism and Human Emotions*. New York: Citadel Press.

Thompson, N (1992) *Existentialism and Social Work*. Aldershot: Avebury.

HUMANISTIC APPROACHES

Headlines

A secular movement within the modernist tradition.

A philosophy for all humanity, the human society.

Humanism values rationality, human rights and freedoms with social responsibility.

Meaning is derived through our relations with other humans.

The quest for knowledge, ethics, art and creativity can all be satisfied through human endeavour.

Introduction to humanistic approaches

In order to appreciate what a humanistic approach to social work might look like, we first need a basic understanding of humanism.

Humanism is a term that embodies a collection of complementary ideas that have varied in prominence throughout history, rather than having been the 'work' of one particular person. The following set of statements are congruent with humanism:

Humans are responsible for themselves and each other; value, worth and dignity is owed to humans, by humans because we are human. The human species is hurtling through the cosmos on a spaceship called Earth. Humans should take care of their home (the planet) for themselves and the people to come. Progress, empirical enquiry and scientific endeavour are encouraged as these are the source of knowledge but with the proviso that the aim should be about improving the quality of human life and well-being. Humanism is then ethical, associating the *end* with the *means* but humanistic ethics is derived by people and not from anywhere else. Human experience is grounded in our common humanity so humanism is atheistic and secular in nature, similar to existentialism. The quality of the life lived by humans and their personal and collective development are important concepts for humanists. Important events in the lives of humanists, such as baby naming, marriage and funerals are celebrated and witnessed (by those invited) and it is life affirming to give recognition to a new life, a union, a life lived without any need of or reference or regard to a deity.

In general terms the values implied in humanism sit very well with the aims and objectives of social work and its intervention. For example, the universal application of human rights and social justice are aspirations both have in common. A comprehensive insight into the association between humanism and social work could be gained by reading Malcolm Payne's book, *Humanistic Social Work*. My book limits the association between humanism and social work to the consideration of person-centred counselling, an intervention commonly identified with humanistic motivation. However, the values and skills required for person-centred counselling provide an excellent template for all professional helping relationships to aspire to. This includes work within the statutory sector where the service user is not a voluntary participant. Adopting the principles underpinning the approach a humanistic counsellor would have to their client does not need to compromise the context of the intervention in, for example, the appropriate discharge of power but it may 'humanise' such an inter-vention. This does not imply that such a practitioner and a humanistic counsellor are interchangeable roles. Specific training and qualifications are required to practise as a counsellor but the practitioner can seek to apply the principles of the skill set of the counsellor in the approach to their service user to work in a person-centred way.

Person-centred counselling

The prefix *person-centred* has come to be ubiquitous in social work, especially within Adult Services where it is used to emphasise the concept that the primary service user is at the centre of service provision and intervention. The term *person-centred working* could be appropriately applied to a broad range of intervention within professional help-ing relationships, provided the work orbits the service user in a manner that adheres to the principles that define the approach. However, the term originates from a specific model of counselling developed by the American psychologist Carl Rogers (1902–1987).

Humanistic psychologists like Rogers thought humans understand their lives in the context of their perceptions of the phenomena they experience as they live their lives. In accord with the strengths-based approach, Rogers asserted that humans have an innate capacity to 'come through' periods of adversity, regenerate and achieve a sense of well-being, especially when given the time and encouragement to do so. He termed this capacity *the actualising tendency* (Mearns and Thorne, 2007, p 12). The term is closely associated with the idea of self-actualisation as proposed by another psychologist, Abraham Maslow, but as this was used to describe the ful-filment of one's potential the terms are complementary. Person-centred counsel-ling is intended to create the environment in which this process can be nurtured. It is a distinct style of counselling, based on a professional relationship in which the counsellor *facilitates* the client's exploration of themselves and their journey, where they are now, where they wish to be. The counsellor, in their role, also undertakes a journey, through the relationship with the client. It is not the same type of journey in that it is not intended to be 'therapeutic' as such but there is a recognition that two humans cannot meet in such a context as counselling without encountering each other; the counsellor cannot remain 'inert' to this experience any more than the client can. Accordingly there is a greater sense of equality between the counsellor and client than that usually found in more traditional *consultative* liaisons. In order to establish and maintain the *person-centredness* style of counselling there are some principles that the counsellor must adopt. Rogers described these as '*core conditions*' (Mearns and Thorne, 2007, p 17).

Rogers's core conditions of person-centred counselling

» **The counsellor is *genuine* and *congruent*.**

They are true to themselves, what the existentialist would describe as being authentic; communicating the concern for their client's well-being is both real and an appropriate 'fit' with the issues they are presented with. There is no façade – 'professional' or otherwise. The concern for the well-being of the client is genuine by dint of them being human, congruent with the orthodoxy of humanism. In a subliminal way the counsellor, in addition to establishing trust, also conveys the notion that it is acceptable to *be yourself*, modelling the idea that people do not have to be someone else to achieve worth or acceptance.

» **The counsellor has *unconditional positive regard* for their client.**

The counsellor views their client positively and respects their autonomy. The quality of the relationship and service offered is not conditional on the 'progress' or otherwise the client is perceived to be making, or any other personal characteristic the client might possess. It is tangibly non-judgemental, creating an environment in which thoughts and feelings can be explored without fear of condemnation. The practitioner will need to make judgements in the course of an assessment and analysis and they need to be both congruent and non-judgemental in so doing. There is no implication that the client's thoughts, feelings or resulting behaviours are beyond challenge, which would potentially be in contradiction of the first core condition. Indeed, their interconnectedness may require examination, but the therapeutic nature of the relationship is not conditional on affect.

» **The counsellor has *empathic understanding* for their client.**

Any counsellor should have well-developed interpersonal skills but the ability to communicate an understanding of another's perception, to 'tune into' what is being communicated to them, how this might feel, and what it may be like to 'be' the person, based on actively listening to what they are being told and checking this out by para-phrasing, which is essential.

These principles are precise, demanding and could be thought of as *setting the bar* for practitioners to aspire to as they are difficult to achieve in a 'complete' sense. They are, to some extent, counter-intuitive to a 'natural' inclination as we *do* judge and form opinions about those we meet, often on little evidence, and can so easily offer advice or interpret what we are hearing to suit our own stance or adapt it to what we might be currently consumed with. Person-centred counselling requires the opposite of such *natural instincts*, irrespective of how well intentioned they might be. The inclin-ation to 'jump in' and to 'right the wrong' has to be resisted. Person-centred counsel-ling requires professional expertise but exercised without the *professional persona*. The skills required to offer this particular intervention, to a competent level, take time to learn, habituate and hone.

The following pictorial representation describes the three positions we can occupy in relating to where *the other* is. The two planes represent different places, where the upper one is more desirable than the other.

Figure 3.1 We are in a different place

Figure 3.2 We are in the same place

Figure 3.3 Enabling moving to a different place

Figure 3.1 could be suggestive of several responses including voyeuristic and critical ones:

I am unable to help.

I am unwilling to help.

I am glad I'm not where you are.

I would not be where you are had similar circumstances occurred for me (because I would have made better decisions).

You deserve to be where you are.

Figure 3.2 could be suggestive of:

I am incapable of helping, or being supportive as I too am hurting, in pain, consumed by or taken up with myself to the extent whereby I don't have the energy or space to be empathetic, resulting in being emotionally unavailable for others.

Figure 3.3 could be suggestive of the context for a professional helping relationship in which the core conditions could apply.

The application of humanistic approaches to social work practice

The values that underpin humanism are broadly congruent with the ethical principles of social work, which include the promotion of human rights and social justice (see BASW's Code of Ethics, 2012). Social workers who consider themselves humanists will hold such principles as universal aspirations but they are also obliged to recognise the importance of culture, religion and creed to people's sense of identity. Difference needs to be acknowledged across a range of diversity in the way humans manifest themselves and is not limited to those of culture and religion. However, where cultural and religious practices deny or undermine human rights and social justice, such as in the practice of female genital mutilation for example, a conflict in values is inevitable. Despite the potential for such conflict, humanistic values offer a theoretical framework for a universal application of social work. However, given the differences in how social work is mandated and practised internationally, the concept of its universal application may remain contentious and for its supporters continue to be largely aspirational.

The application of a humanistic approach as exemplified through person-centred counselling is a specific intervention which lies predominantly within the field of personal counselling. However, the principles that guide person-centred counselling provide a sound ethical basis for any relationship-based, professional helping service. There are contextual considerations which, at first glance, may draw this assertion into question. For example, can a social worker in a youth offending team have *unconditional positive regard* for the young offender they are formally supervising through a court order? Surely, one might say, in such statutory interventions the social worker has additional factors to consider such as whether or not their service user re-offends while subject to the supervision order. This is, of course, true and a substantive factor to the outcome of the intervention, but ethically the social worker can and should maintain unconditional positive regard in their approach to their service user as it is the positive regard for them as a human being and their service user that is unconditional, and is not dependent on their behaviour. The professional application of unconditional positive regard does not deny the social worker expressing disapproval for certain behaviours such as re-offending. As they are required to be genuine and congruent in their relationship with the service user, they should be open and honest in how they 'experienced' the service user and their behaviour. In the example, the social worker would explore the re-offending behaviour and encourage their service user to understand why it occurred but in a non-judgemental way.

Let's consider how a humanistic approach might be applied to the case study we are working with.

Case study

The presenting circumstances have not changed. Annette is a white 23-year-old woman with two children: a baby, Sam, aged 18 months, and a toddler, Ben aged two and a half. They live in a small rural town. Her current partner, Andy, is an intravenous drug user who lives part of the time at Annette's; the rest of the time he spends at friends who live in a bigger town some 30 miles away. Sam and Ben are considered 'children in need' as defined in the 1989 Children Act.

The prominence humanism gives to the concepts of human rights and social justice enables a humanistic perspective to sit well with the principles of good social work practice. Social work intervention with Annette, Andy and the children that would embody both humanistic principles and those which constitute good social work practice would include:

» the incorporation of the core conditions in the approach the practitioner takes to working with Annette, Andy and Ben and Sam. For while the practitioner is not offering person-centred counselling, they can apply person-centred working;

» practising in ways that facilitate, mobilise and develop Annette's and Andy's experiences, knowledge and skills;

» seeking to develop Annette's sense of personal growth and self-concept (including that of Andy as appropriate); help them to identify goals and support them in the achievement of these;

» promoting their human rights and those of her children.

(Adapted from Payne, 2011, p 29)

Although the social worker's primary service users are Ben and Sam and their welfare is the primary consideration, there is nothing to prevent the principles of person-centred working being applied to the work undertaken with Annette and Andy; in fact, there is everything to be gained. Employing the core conditions could establish an optimal basis for engagement, especially where there is potential for service users to perceive some degree of condemnation due to the need for the involvement of social care. The demonstration of unconditional positive regard to those whose experience of anything like acceptance has been entirely conditional can be transformative. If Annette feels as though she may be judged as a mum, she is unlikely to share her thoughts and feelings about the times when she can't be bothered with the kids and when they stress her out. If these times cannot be discussed then strategies to manage them cannot be either. An empathetic understanding of what it might be like to be Annette could enable Annette to share this. Unless Annette feels it is safe enough to allow some access to her world, then exploring what else her world could contain is unlikely to happen.

Relationship-based social work

The presence of the core conditions is a pre-requisite for relationship-based social work. It may seem unnecessary to stress the importance of establishing a relationship as a basis for motivating change in social work intervention as it could be regarded as *going without saying*. All the more reason to say it! What happens in the lives of the four people has got to matter to the social worker and in a manner that can be conveyed to the four people concerned. At its simplest, service user feedback following intervention in which the service user said *'my social worker cared about what happened to me'* is likely to have been successful intervention. It is certainly indicative of a positive interaction. This is what the essence of *use of self* amounts to and calls for an affective dimension, an emotional demand upon the social worker in any intervention. The core conditions specifically address the potential pitfalls for which traditional case working has attracted criticism; 'pathologising' the service user through the power imbalance of the professional's expertise. The core conditions can reduce the potential for a defensive reaction to the proposed intervention on the part of the service user. However, there would be no substitute for finding out what Annette and Andy think of the prospect of social work intervention and how they feel about having a social worker as this may need to be addressed as past experiences and or negative associations could hinder engagement. It may be useful to establish some parameters for the involvement so as to keep in check any fear and anxiety involvement may provoke.

For a comprehensive, theoretical analysis of relationship-based social work see Gillian Ruch et al's book of the same name. The authors propose a model of working which is characterised by the following assertions:

> » *Human behaviours and the professional relationship are an integral component of any professional intervention.*

> » *Human behaviour is complex and multifaceted. People are not simply rational beings but have affective (both conscious and unconscious) dimensions that enrich but simultaneously complicate human relationships.*

> » *The internal and external worlds of individuals are inseparable, so integrated (psychosocial), as opposed to one-dimensional, responses to social problems are crucial for social work practice.*

> » *Each social work encounter is unique and attention must be paid to the specific circumstances of each individual.*

> » *A collaborative relationship is the means through which interventions are channelled, and this requires a particular emphasis to be placed on the 'use of self'.*

> » *The respect for individuals embedded in relationship-based practice involves practising in inclusive and empowering ways.*

(Ruch et al, 2010, p 21)

Uncharacteristic of the approaches introduced in this book, the model represents a hybrid, combining ideas from psycho-dynamic and psycho-social traditions with person-centred working. There would be little to be gained from attempting to be prescriptive about optimal or minimal durations of involvement, other than to suggest an intervention should be of sufficient duration for an outcome to its objectives to be established and support offered while any 'new' behaviours are habituated. Unlike brief solution work, relationship-based social work requires sufficient time to establish a relationship but this need not exclude short-term interventions as it would depend on the participants as to whether a relationship was established and if so whether it was of sufficient quality to be of influence.

Some personal reflections on intervention drawing on the ideas from a humanistic approach

In his book, *Humanistic Social Work*, Malcolm Payne asserts that the application of humanistic principles in social work is underused and their potential understated. This may well be the case but the problem is there are few techniques that can be applied that could be described as *humanistic* as the principles embody a philosophical stance and inform personal values rather than a procedure but this is the strength of this approach. Humanistic principles offer the social worker an additional safeguard for ethical practice and a means by which busy social workers can health check and if necessary 'spring clean' their values and the manner in which they regard service users. It is difficult to discriminate against someone you regard as an equal. Person-centred working offers a benchmark standard for engagement, and relationship-based social work, as far as I am concerned, makes the difference in every sense of the word. If there is any doubt about this, consider what has characterised those who have 'made a difference' in your own life. For me it would be that there was something significant in the relationship we had.

The upholding of human rights

Although not an *intervention* as such, a registered social worker is both legally and morally obliged to promote and uphold the human rights of their service users. The Human Rights Act 1998 contains 14 articles that set out the rights that people who live in the UK can justly claim. We will consider two of these that have particular significance for Annette, Ben and Sam but firstly the concepts of *rights* and *natural justice* in general terms merit consideration.

It could be reasonably argued that a biological parent has a moral right to bring up their children (providing that doing so does not compromise the welfare of the children). It could equally be argued that children have a moral right to be brought up by their parents (with the same caveat). It could also be argued that preventing these moral rights (without a good and lawful reason) would be contrary to the notion of *natural justice*. Unsurprisingly, these 'moral rights' and the notion of *natural justice* are safeguarded by being enshrined in the UK's primary legislation: Section (1) (3) of the Children Act 1989 provides for '*parental responsibility*' to be conferred on the parent of a child, allowing the parent to bring up the child to the exclusion of those without it. Even where children are considered 'in need' of services to ensure they have an opportunity to achieve a reasonable standard of health and development, there is a legal requirement that authorities promote the upbringing of such children by their families (Section 17 (1) (b) Children Act, 1989).

In addition to the legal provisions in the Children Act, article 3 and 8 of the Human Rights Act are also relevant.

Article 8: *Right to respect for private and family life*

Everyone has the right to respect for their private and family life, their home and their correspondence.

This article is qualified thus:

There shall be no interference by a public authority with the exercise of this right except such as is in accordance with the law and is necessary in a democratic society in the interests of national security, public safety or the economic well-being of the country, for the prevention of disorder or crime, for the protection of health or morals, or for the protection of the rights and freedoms of others.

Article 3: *Prohibition of torture*

No one shall be subjected to torture or to inhuman or degrading treatment or punishment.

This article is not qualified. It is absolute.

In cases where children are subjected to severe and persistent neglect, which of course could include Ben and Sam if the extent to which their needs were met deteriorated or failed to improve, they are subject to inhuman or degrading treatment, contrary to article 3. So, in order to uphold this absolute right, article 8 could be lawfully breached, in that Annette could be subject to interference by a public authority (social services) under the qualification of protecting the rights and freedoms of Ben and Sam.

There is adequate provision through parts IV and V of the Children Act 1989 to protect children without recourse to the Human Rights Act to safeguard their welfare but the articles make important statements about the rights British citizens (of all ages) can legitimately claim from the state. In the example of Annette and her children, they illustrate how the rights conferred through the Human Rights Act have the potential to conflict and give comparable status to minors to that of adults.

References and further reading

British Association of Social Workers (BASW) (2012) *The Code of Ethics for Social Work: Statement of Principles*. Birmingham: British Association of Social Workers. [online] Available at: http://cdn.basw.co.uk/upload/basw_95243-9.pdf (accessed 24 March 2017).

Children Act 1989 (c.41). London: TSO. [online] Available at: www.legislation.gov.uk/ukpga/1989/41/contents (accessed 24 March 2017).

Howe, D (2013) *Empathy: What It Is and Why It Matters*. Basingstoke: Palgrave Macmillan.

Human Rights Act 1998 (c.42). London: TSO. [online] Available at: www.legislation.gov.uk/ukpga/1998/42/contents (accessed 24 March 2017).

Mearns, D and Thorne, B (2007) *Person-Centred Counselling in Action* (3rd ed). London: Sage.

Payne, M (2011) *Humanistic Social Work: Core Principles in Practice*. Basingstoke: Palgrave Macmillan.

Parrish, M (2010) *Social Work Perspectives on Human Behaviour*. Maidenhead: Open University Press.

Rogers, C (1961) *On Becoming a Person*. Boston: Houghton Mifflin Publishers.

Ruch, G, Turney, D and Ward, A (2010) *Relationship-based Social Work*. London: Jessica Kingsley Publishers.

PROBLEM-SOLVING APPROACHES

Headlines

Forget about causes and the past.

Focused, purposeful, time-limited interventions.

Inclined towards the practical, appeals to activists (learning styles).

A 'sleeves rolled up' approach which has direct links to the issues.

Can be a negotiated, contract-based form of intervention.

Just do it!

Introduction to problem-solving approaches

Much of the impetus for the development of problem-solving approaches is attributed to the work of Helen Perlman, a social work academic from the University of Chicago and who, in 1957, published *Social Casework: A Problem-Solving Process.* Perlman observed that while problems could be contextualised holistically, they had to be broken down into their constituent parts to be worked on. This idea underpins the basis for problem-solving approaches (Healy, 2014, p 138).

Another notion this approach drew into contestation was the duration of the intervention. How long should a service user have a social worker for? An easy answer would be to say it depends on the service user's needs, or the context for intervention. A more considered analysis of the question however reveals its complexity and why this is a vexed question for the social work profession which is not asked often enough. A parent who, through early-life deprivation, remains needy of nurture and parenting themselves may require long-term support in which the social worker could become akin to a social relative for intervention to be effective. The vulnerable service user, who has poor social capital, may need long-term support while engaging in a process of change and early maintenance.

Critics of long-term support point to the risk of developing dependency in, perhaps not solely, the service user and creating 'professional clients', arguing that it's not 'normal' to have a social worker as a means of support. But in the absence of anyone else, why not?

We do not consider those fortunate enough to have a rich pool of supportive family and friends to call on over-catered for do we? But they are less likely to have social workers. However, extending social work intervention beyond that which could be achieved in a shorter time could not be justified in either ethical or economic terms. Research-based practice may help inform such considerations although determining a ratio of time-scales to outcomes is problematic due to the number of determinates involved. Perhaps the debate is a non-starter given the pressure on case load numbers and the need to allocate cases irrespective of whether or not the worker has sufficient time to undertake the work they warrant in a meaningful way. In any event, problem-solving approaches sidestep such deliberations by focusing intervention on *the problem* as perceived and defined and devising a time-limited, goal-orientated programme to address it.

Problem-solving approaches have appeal for the social worker and the service user in that intervention is:

> » Targeted:
>   On ameliorating or eradicating the problem, as defined by the social worker, with input from the service user, or defined by the service user with input from the social worker, depending on who initiates the intervention but *the target* should be a product of negotiation.

> » Tangible:
>   Concrete objectives and goals are set out and agreed in a manner in which expectations of who is doing what are identified.

> » Transparent:
>   The *road map* routing the intervention including review and evaluation is visible and devoid of 'hidden agendas'.

> » Time-limited:
>   The intervention is time-limited. It has a defined beginning and end. Even where it is agreed that the intervention is extended it will be subject to the same structure as opposed to being *open-ended*.

Any intervention that seeks to identify and address a problem in a systematised, time-limited way could be described as a problem-solving approach. For the purposes of this book two particular methods will be considered. The first is task-centred practice and the second is solution-focused brief therapy.

Task-centred practice

Two American social work academics, William Reid and Laura Epstein, writing in the 1970s developed the methodology of problem-solving intervention in their book

Task-Centred Casework, published in 1972. It proved a ground-breaking text offering the social worker a pragmatic method of intervention with clear, comprehensible aims and objectives. As it is a highly structured method of intervention it can be represented as a series of stages or phases. Reid, as reproduced in Malcolm Payne's book *Modern Social Work Theory*, identified ten stages (Payne, 2005, p 112). Peter Marsh and Mark Doel identified twelve stages in their publication, *The Task-centred Book* (Marsh and Doel, 2005, p 15). Karen Healy cited eight key principles of task-centred practice in her book, *Social Work Theories in Context* (Healy, 2014, p 142). Rather than simply replicating each of these, what follows is a generic structure, informed by the sources referenced but reduced to four sequential phases.

1. Establish the rationale for intervention.

2. Define the problems to be addressed.

3. Identify and apportion tasks to address the problems.

3A. Set out in writing what has been agreed and implement it.

4. Review and evaluate the intervention.

Phase 1: Establish the rationale for intervention

At the time of writing (1972), Reid devised the technique of task-centred practice for a voluntary service user group, committed to social work intervention. One may regard such service users as *optimal* in terms of prospects for engagement and outcome. However, the technique was soon to be applied to a broad range of service users, including those who may be described as involuntary, the result of statutory intervention. In either event it is important to establish the rationale for the intervention, including the legal duties and powers of the agency involved. As with any intervention, consideration needs to be given to the appropriateness of obtaining the service user's informed consent to the proposed intervention. In any event, what is being proposed should be explained and the anticipated involvement understood. If the matters at issue have the potential to lead to consequences not currently apparent such as legal proceedings, it is important that the social worker is 'upfront' about this. Workers who are rightly concerned with the potential for intervention to become coercive have to counter this by ensuring they discharge their power appropriately, and be mindful that under a *no surprises* principle, in practice it would be unethical to conceal this risk where it was a realistic possibility.

Phase 2: Define the problems to be addressed

This is a crucial element to the outcome of the intervention. Even if desired, if the problem to be addressed is unlikely to be achieved or it falls outside of what the service user *can* or has the power to address, it should not be included as it is setting the service user up to fail. The aim of defining problems is to turn them into objectives so they must be addressable.

The degree of precision in establishing an understanding of 'the problem' needs to be forensic. For example, if the problem (as defined by Malcolm's mum) is Malcolm's behaviour towards her, then this is insufficiently specific to be worked with. Further 'drilling down' into 'the problem' reveals that Malcolm's mum feels he is disrespectful towards her. This is still inadequate, as when we convert this into a task, we are left with asking Malcolm to be more respectful to his mum. That's like asking a child to be 'better behaved' and is sufficiently imprecise to be ignored. Finally, the particular aspect of Malcolm's disrespectful behaviour towards his mum is identified: he swears at her. Now we know the problem behaviour. However, we need to know the *incidence* of the behaviour as once per month is different to once per day. This consideration is not intended to imply that some less frequent incidence of Malcolm swearing at his mum is acceptable but we need to know the dimensions of the problem. If we were undertaking task-centred intervention with Malcolm and his mum, we would also need to hear from Malcolm. Malcolm, who is 11 years old, complained that his mum rarely spends any time with him since she took up with Dave 18 months ago. A similar degree of specificity need to be applied to Malcolm's problem as to his mum's. The worker needs to establish *what* they did together then that they are not doing now, how often and to then consider what would be appropriate to do together now.

It is possible that the problems identified to be addressed are the result of a bargaining process by the parties involved. For example, in a safeguarding case the social worker might have one or more 'non-negotiable' problems to be addressed. However, it would feel like an abuse of power if this wasn't offset in some way by including something that the service user wanted. Although different parties can bring different problems, a preparedness to work on those that are agreed by the parties to be worked on is necessary.

Phase 3: Identify and apportion tasks to address the problems

This is where the final sentence of the previous paragraph begins to be tested out. The problems identified and agreed to be addressed are converted into tasks and apportioned to those responsible for addressing them and by when. So, if we return to Malcolm and his mum, his mum has agreed to watch a film with him once per week, starting Thursday next week (as an exclusive activity between them). He is to stop swearing at her, also from next week. There may be additional problems to be addressed and they might include Dave in a real case but it is advised that the number of tasks reflect some degree of balance between the parties and that there are few rather than many. A maximum of two or three tasks each is sensible initially to see how this goes, to give the parties the opportunities to succeed and gain confidence in the process, and to start to habituate the 'new' behaviour into something they can see the benefit of doing. It is worth being mindful of the SMART acronym as objectives have a better chance to be met if they are:

» Specific

» Measurable

» Achievable

» Realistic

» Timely

(Doran, 1981)

Phase 3A: Set out what has been agreed in writing and implement it

This is phase 3A rather than 4 because it is the culmination of phase 3, between apportioning the tasks and implementation. Those involved may decide to orally agree only but committing to a written agreement, especially if signatures are included, can give the agreement added gravitas. Each party to the agreement signs the agreed version and they have their own copy. Using written agreements when utilising task-centred practice is common within statutory intervention. They can be authoritarian and perfunctory or personal and creative. For example, see the written agreement in Figure 3.4:

A written agreement between xxx (name of service user) and x local authority	
xxx (name of service user) agrees to undertake the following tasks by (date)	
Task one described	
Task two described	
Task three described	
Task four described	
Signed xxx (service user)	(date)
xxx (social worker)	(date)
This written agreement will be reviewed on	(date)

Figure 3.4 An example of using written agreements in an authoritarian manner

This is a basic form but it is impersonal and can represent little more than a list of stipulations for the service user to comply with, which does little to foster co-operation and create a spirit of joint endeavour. It fails to say anything about how early success might be recognised or allude to what would happen in the event of non-compliance.

A written agreement between xxx (service user) and xxx (social worker)	
xxx (service user) and xxx (social worker) agree to undertake the following tasks	
Tasks for xxx (service user)	
Task one described	(date)
Task two described	(date)
Task three described	(date)
Tasks for xxx (social worker)	
Task one described	(date)
Task two described	(date)
Early success by xxx (service user) will be recognised by (reward activity chosen by service user)	
Non-compliance will trigger xxx eg an early review of agreement	
Signed xxx (service user)	(date)
xxx (social worker)	(date)
This written agreement will be reviewed on	(date)

Figure 3.5 An example of using written agreements in a manner which demonstrates working in partnership

In the form in Figure 3.5, the social worker is named as the other party rather than the local authority, making it more personal. Including some tasks for the social worker gives the agreement a sense of a joint enterprise, demonstrating partnership working. The tasks for the social worker do not have to equate with those of the service user. There is a difference in power and it is usually helpful if this is acknowledged. It is important that the service user understands what will happen in the event of non-compliance. It is also important to mark early success.

Phase 4: Review and evaluate the intervention

Reviewing and evaluating any intervention is an important part of the ASPIRE model (Sutton, 2006) (assess, plan, intervene, review and evaluate). It provides an opportunity to recognise what has been achieved and, no less significant, what has not. It may be that while not fully achieved there has been sufficient progress for a compromise to be reached and the objective to be considered met. Where an objective has not been met or insufficiently so as to enable a compromise, some consideration as to why and what needs to happen as a result is necessary. There may be a variety of reasons why one or more tasks have not resulted in sustained change. The task or tasks may have been poorly chosen and represent some over-ambition on the part of the worker or the service user or both. Another's influence may be undermining or sabotaging the intervention, in which case consideration needs to be given to the merits of making them a party to the agreement. Alternatively, it may be the result of non-compliance which may, in some forms of statutory intervention, nudge the involvement towards legal proceedings.

Although task-centred practice may, in such cases, be thought to have failed, the intervention remains entirely worthwhile as it will have presented the service user with an opportunity to avoid such consequences (which is why it is important to state the likely consequences of non-compliance at the outset) and it demonstrates the efforts the agency has made to work in partnership and avoid such proceedings. It may be decided that a further period of intervention is undertaken, re-visiting some adapted tasks and/or new ones. In these circumstances, the 'extended' intervention may again be subject to the structured approach and a new written agreement. Where the task-centred intervention has resulted in 'new' or changed behaviour, the social worker should enquire as to what support is required and available to help the service user maintain and habituate the changed behaviour as the social worker's involvement is likely to end.

The problem with 'problems'

Even where we have 'problems' we can be reluctant to 'own' them, especially where others assert we have them rather than ourselves. It's as though we could be tainted by association with the term so denial may be a better way to keep ourselves intact even though this may risk repeating behaviours which may not be in our best interests. If, momentarily, we recall psycho-dynamic theory, Freud identified this phenomenon and went on to describe several *defence mechanisms*, some of which, especially denial, fit well into the thinking here. Labelling theory is also relevant, as is the use of language in constructing our perception in creating an identifying association between the person and the problem. Using an alternative to the word *problem* is not really going to work as if it is to 'take on' the meaning we give to the difficulties we mean when we talk of problems it will accrue 'problemness' no matter what we call it. So why not do away with it altogether...?

Solution-focused brief therapy

This approach is attributed to the work of S de Shazer and colleagues who worked at the Brief Family Therapy Center in the USA in the 1980s (Brief Family Therapy Center, 2007). The idea behind the approach is simple enough: rather than the therapy seeking to address 'problems' (which, in an open-ended course of treatment could develop into something ongoing), the focus is on what the client wants to achieve as a result of the therapy. Such a focus concentrates the minds of both client and therapist and enables the engagement to be brief.

Barbra Teater, in her book *Applying Social Work Theories and Methods*, cites the work of Walter and Peller, who identified a number of assumptions that characterise solution-focused work, seven of which are:

1 Focus on solutions

2 There are always exceptions to 'the problem'

3 Change is normal

4 Small changing leads to larger changing

5 Clients cooperate with solutions they can work with

6 People already possess what they need to solve their problems

7 Intervention is goal oriented

(Teater, 2014, p 173)

Siobhan Maclean and Rob Harrison, in their book *Social Work Theory*, broadly concur with Walter and Peller, describing six elements of solution-focussed intervention:

» A belief that people can develop strategies to address the difficulties they face.

» Empowering people to identify and apply their own solutions works.

» Intervention is dominated by building workable answers, not the 'problems'.

» The counsellor crafts questions that draw out and build on the service user's strengths.

» The intervention is directed to the present/future.

» The counselling relationship is goal-orientated; the goals being:

a. generated by the service user;

b. small rather than large;

c. described in specific concrete, behavioural terms;

d. realistic and achievable.

They go on to identify the types of questions used in solution-focused brief therapy (SFBT) cited in the fourth element:

Goal-setting questions

For example, exploring what the service user hopes to achieve as a result of the intervention.

The 'miracle' question

This question invites the service user to imagine and describe what their life would be like if their difficulties were to miraculously disappear; how would they recognise this? What would this mean for them?

Scaling questions

A commonly used tool in most problem-solving interventions and a feature in the Signs of Safety approach are scaling questions. Such questions are asked to quantify the service user's perception of the difficulty they are experiencing and to set a bench-mark against which progress can be measured. For example, with someone suffering from an anxiety disorder the practitioner may ask: *'On a scale of 1 to 10 (where 1 is minimal and 10 is maximal), how would you score the amount of time you have been anxious in the past week?'* If the service user scored 5, this would represent 50 per cent of the time. There are 168 hours in a week, so for 84 of these the service user described themselves as anxious, which also means that for the other 84 that com-prised that week they were not. The practitioner could ask the service user to main-tain a diary for the next week and note the periods in which they were anxious and then see how that compared with the first score. It would be unusual for the service user to underestimate the original score, so unless the forthcoming week is atypical the score is likely to be lower. In this way the practitioner and the service user can gain an idea of the perceived dimensions of the problem and by comparing this to the diary, gain an evidence-based idea of its actual size.

In SFBT the practitioner might frame the scaling question: *'How would you score the amount of time you have been calm in the past week?'* Assuming the same score of 5 is given, they can point out that for 50 per cent of the time the service user is managing their condition and could then go on to use a coping question to explore how they are managing to do this.

Exception-finding questions

These questions ask the service user to identify times when the *presenting issue* was not present. This is then used to serve as a platform from which to identify and explore strategies the service user is currently employing and how these might be bolstered and extended.

Coping questions

These questions enable the service user to recognise their own strengths, capabilities and resourcefulness in managing their situation.

For example, the practitioner may ask the service user: '*Given the difficulties you have recently been facing, how have you managed to cope so well with your day-to-day responsibilities?*' This type of question prompts the service user to acknowledge the abilities they are currently deploying as opposed to the difficulties their presenting issues are causing.

(Maclean and Harrison, 2008, p 147)

The application of problem-solving approaches to social work practice

The methods of intervention associated with problem-solving approaches were originally developed from work with service users who sought therapeutic help, usually through a counselling relationship and so were voluntary service users. However, elements from these approaches could be applied to involuntary service users and such initiatives could prove especially helpful where 'problems' are long-standing and practitioners feel 'stuck' as to how best to move forward. The mandate for statutory intervention does not exclude the practitioner using a solution-focused approach. The only adaptation might be the addition of the practitioner's agenda in addition to that of the service user's. It would be informative to explore where 'common ground' lay between what the practitioner and what the service user would regard as *progress* and ultimately what a successful outcome to intervention would look like. For example, in statutory intervention, concern for the welfare of a child may be one thing that the practitioner and the child's carer could coalesce around as something they had in common. A mutual objective of the intervention could be identified as the intervention being no longer necessary. If that indeed was how the service user would define success, small steps towards achieving it could be identified, converted into tasks and implemented. In this way a service user who was initially reluctant to engage could become more amenable to it through seeing the objectives of the intervention, *where it was going* and have some responsibility for bringing it to an end.

Let's see how these two methods of intervention from a problem-solving approach might be applied to the case study we have been working with.

Firstly, a recap on the circumstances:

Case study

Annette is a white 23-year-old woman with two children: a baby, Sam, aged 18 months and a toddler, Ben, aged two and a half. They live in a small rural town. Her current partner, Andy, is an intravenous drug user who lives part of the time at Annette's; the rest of the time he spends at friends who live in a bigger town some 30 miles away. Sam and Ben are considered 'children in need' as defined in the 1989 Children Act and the social worker has begun a number of visits to update an assessment of how the children's needs are being met and to monitor the children's welfare and their home environment, both of which have been neglected at times. The house shows signs of neglect and there are issues around hygiene; the social worker noticed a pile of dirty nappies heaped up in a corner of the living room. Annette's apparent 'open door' policy results in a number of people coming and going and on a previous visit the social worker noticed a number of people congregated in the home, two of whom she knew should have been at school. The supervision and some personal care of the children such as feeding and nappy changing appears to be quite disorganised and undertaken by a number of people.

The application of task-centred practice

The social worker is visiting Annette for the third time and had asked that Andy be there as she wanted to propose a method of intervention that would require the co-operation of both Annette and Andy and the involvement of all three of them. The social worker had avoided taking a personal history and did not discuss the agency's previous involvement. She said that on the two previous visits, during which she had assessed how the needs of the children were being met, she had seen some things she was worried about. She wanted to share these things and to ask Annette and Andy if they would be prepared to work with her to address them, as they would result in improvements for Ben and Sam which, if adopted and maintained, would lead to the end of social care's involvement. She recognised that so far this had sounded all one-way and proposed that they identify some things that she may be able to help with or support them in achieving these changes.

The social worker said that her worries included concerns for the health and safety of Ben and Sam, the number of people who undertake their personal care such as nappy changing and the likely consequences for the quality of the relationships they have with Annette and Andy. She said that these were the reasons why Ben and Sam were considered in need of services from social care and that she would not be able to simply continue to be concerned for their welfare during the progress of their childhood; she wanted to see the change that would bring her involvement to an end rather than it continuing and becoming more intrusive. Annette asked what she meant by this and the worker said if there was evidence of continued neglect, she would have to consider changing the children's status from being in need of services to that of in need of protection but added that this could easily be avoided by giving a few undertakings, upholding them and doing a few things differently. Annette and Andy said they wanted to know more about these undertakings and the 'few things'. The social worker proposed identifying these into tasks that she would expect Annette and Andy to carry out, adding that they too could identify things that they wanted from her and she would consider if she could take these on as tasks for her to carry out also. Further discussion took place specifying the 'few things' into observable behaviours, which were converted into objectives in a written agreement between the parties. It was agreed that the parties would only sign and activate the written agreement when they thought the objectives and timescales set out in it were ones they were happy with and considered achievable. Below is a copy of the written agreement (note: all names are fictitious).

A written agreement between Annette Nash, Andy Naylor and Adele Norris (social worker)
Annette, Andy and Adele agree to undertake the following tasks:
Tasks for Annette and Andy
Drug/substance usage
No dealing of illegal drugs is to take place from the home address of Ben and Sam from 01/ 11/2016
Ben and Sam should not be in the room when drugs are used. They should not have access to the drugs or any equipment associated with drug-taking from 01/11/2016
Either Annette or Andy will ensure they are capable of supervising Sam and Ben when they have responsibility for their care from 01/11/2016
Childcare
Annette or Andy are primarily responsible for the care and supervision of Ben and Sam. They should undertake the majority of their feeding, changing their nappies, bathing and putting to bed. Only people closely associated with Ben and Sam should undertake these tasks from 01/11/2016

The home
Schoolchildren should not be allowed to visit the home when they should be at school
Rubbish including dirty nappies should be disposed of in the dustbin outside the house from 01/11/2016
Tasks for Adele (social worker)
Adele will liaise with the housing about the longstanding rent arrears that built up during her last period of employment and try to negotiate a reduction and a payment plan by 08/11/2016
Adele will make enquiries about a local credit union and find out how Annette might join by 08/11/2016
Early success by Annette and Andy will be recognised by Adele organising childcare for an evening, enabling them to go out to celebrate Annette's forthcoming birthday by 29/11/2016
Annette and Andy will notify Adele if either are not upholding these undertakings. If Adele finds that these undertakings are not being upheld she will bring forward a review of this agreement and consider what needs to happen, dependent on the consequences for Ben and Sam

Signed	Annette Nash	date	01/11/2016
	Andy Naylor	date	01/11/2016
	Adele Norris	date	01/11/2016
This written agreement will be reviewed on		date	13/12/2016

The rationale for some of the social worker's non-negotiable tasks should be given so as to aid compliance. For example, faecal matter from the nappies can cause infections and diseases, including blindness. Annette and Andy are encouraged to undertake the personal care of Ben and Sam to aid their attachment to the children and the attachment the children have to their primary carers, in addition to any safeguarding considerations.

The review would consider how the agreement is working for its signatories. The need for its continuation and any changes that need to be made to it are also considered before any summative evaluation of the intervention is made. It may be that this form of intervention suits Annette and Andy and they may engage in a new agreement that sets other objectives the signatories wish to address. In the event of evidence that the tasks are not being undertaken by those assigned to undertake them, any of the signatories can request an early review of the agreement. In the event of the intervention failing to bring about any improvement to the care and supervision of Ben and Sam, the agreement forms part of the evidence the social worker can provide to demonstrate the attempts the local authority made to work in partnership and promote the upbringing of children in need by their families, should such evidence be needed in the future.

The application of solution-focused brief therapy

Intervention under this approach could start with an exploration of what Annette and Andy would identify as desirable outcomes of any intervention, and what they would seek to change, if they could, about the various aspects of which their lives were comprised. Because the intervention is driven by a need to safeguard and promote the welfare of Ben and Sam, the social worker would also have an *agenda* that would need to be included in the work with Annette and Andy. However, that does not preclude the worker adopting an empowering approach and instilling in Annette and or Andy that they possess the ability to formulate coping mechanisms and solutions to the issues they face. The social worker could devise a series of questions, as illustrated earlier, to draw out existing strengths and identify stepping stones towards change.

This exploration would firstly seek to determine what was working well and what was working well enough in Annette and Andy's world. Recognition of the specific skills and abilities would be given that bring this about. In this way the social worker can help establish a ratio of perceived strengths that can prevent the need for change dominating the intervention. Even issues that have the potential to be contentious could be worked with. For example, it may be the case that Annette and Andy regard recreational alcohol and drug usage as a pleasurable and valued coping mechanism and behaviour they do not seek to change. It may well be unrealistic for the social worker to seek to change this but they could look at protective factors that are or could be put in place so the children's vulnerability is not increased at such times by ensuring they have access to substitute care, or someone responsible and capable of appropriate care and supervision at such times.

References and further reading

Brief Family Therapy Center (2007) *Solutions since 1982*. Milwaukee, USA: Brief Family Therapy Center. [online] Available at: www.sfbta.org/bftc/steve_de_shazer_insoo_kim_burg.html (accessed 24 March 2017).

Doran, G (1981) There's a S.M.A.R.T. Way to Write Management's Goals and Objectives. *Management Review*, 70(11): 35–6.

Healy, K (2005) *Social Work Theories in Context*. Basingstoke: Palgrave Macmillan.

Maclean, S and Harrison, R (2008) *Social Work Theory: A Straightforward Guide for Practice Assessors and Placement Supervisors*. Rugeley: Kirwin Maclean Associates Ltd.

Marsh, P and Doel, M (2005) *The Task-centred Book*. Abingdon: Routledge.

Payne, M (2005) *Modern Social Work Theory*. Basingstoke: Palgrave Macmillan.

Perlman, H (1957) *Social Casework: A Problem-solving Process*. Chicago: Chicago University Press.

Reid, W and Epstein, L (1972) *Task-Centred Casework*. New York: Columbia University Press.

Sutton, C (2006) *Helping Families with Troubled Children: A Preventative Approach* (2nd ed). Oxford: Wiley.

Teater, B (2014) *Applying Social Work Theories and Methods* (2nd ed). Maidenhead: Open University Press.

Chapter 4

Pick 'n' mix: the integration of theory and approach in holistic practice

So, there we have it, as far as this publication is concerned. In further reading you may come across additional theories and approaches but these tend to be derivatives of the main ideas that have been introduced.

A quick recap

Psycho-dynamic theory holds that, at a subconscious level, the quality of past experiences are important factors which influence the present and future. Through child development and the life course a series of stages are presented which need to be traversed. The extent to which these are 'successfully' traversed impacts one's personality. Where the 'challenges' within the stages are not satisfactorily resolved or effectively managed, neuroses may result. Analytical access to this drama can only be gained through an intermediary such as a psychotherapist.

Behaviourist theory holds that human behaviour and its motivation is subject to stimulation that prompt responses which can be manipulated through reward as reinforcement. It is a transparent mechanism amenable to an operative making adjustments which result in changed behaviour.

Systems theory holds that the 'product' is a result of the function (or not) of an interconnected system or systems and that changing one or more of these functions results in a different 'product' or outcome.

Radical theory claims that it is the inherent inequality and unfairness in the distribution of wealth, power and opportunity between people that results in the social problems we see in our societies. In terms of an intervention with a specific service user as opposed to that directed towards the community, there is little a social worker can do other than to acknowledge the life chances they consider themselves to have had.

The approaches move away from the more deterministic world of theory, of cause and effect, and tend to adopt a less authoritative juxtaposition between the practitioner and service user.

Strengths-based approaches focus on the assertion that we each have the capacity to heal, grow and develop. One's confidence in this capacity may be buried or bruised but the aim of the professional is to help nurture the environment where this capacity can be revealed and flourish.

Existential approaches. Existentialism denies us the opportunity to 'run for cover' provided by excuses. We are solely responsible for ourselves and the quest for the existentialist is to become authentic (one version of ourselves in which our beliefs and behaviours are in focus). We are free-falling within our existence, free (and condemned) to become who and what we choose. It is a scary liberation.

Humanistic/person-centred approaches. Closely allied to existentialism, Humanism holds that as human beings we *are* 'all in this together' and there is nothing we can know that lies outside of human experience. This begs the question of why, as a species, can we not all get on a little better with each other? We have some way to go with this idea but meanwhile the humanistic principles of person-centred work hold out a universal way of relating to each other.

Problem-solving approaches seek to do just that! They rely on identifying the presenting issues and their corresponding solutions. Interventions using this approach are characterised by their relatively restricted focus, which while having the potential to be refreshing, take no account of *underlying causes*.

What works for you? What works for your service user? What worked for me?

The first two questions are for you and your service user. However, if you have not already established preferences it is likely that you will, but try to resist shutting down options as this will result in reducing what might work for the service user. As I cannot answer these questions I will share what I consider 'worked' for me but it is the responsibility of each practitioner to select and hone their skills in applying the theory, approach and methods of intervention they think appropriate.

As a qualified social worker I undertook statutory work, initially *patch-based*, generic social work, later specialising in working with children and their families.

Contributions from psycho-dynamic theory

Early in the intervention (perhaps the second or third visit), I would invariably take a personal history. This presents the service user with the opportunity to say what has happened to them; to provide a narrative account of what they have experienced. This is useful in a number of ways:

» It can be therapeutic for its own sake.

» It can be a unique source of additional information.

» It can present the worker with the opportunity to:

1. Listen;

2. Build rapport;

3. Demonstrate interest in the service user and their past;

4. Say why this could be of interest in the context of the intervention;

5. Say what will happen to any information shared;

6. Discover an affective dimension: *'How did you feel about that?'*

7. Gain an idea about the service user's insights into their past;

8. Gain an idea about what the service user is prepared to share with you;

9. Gain an idea about how any previous social work involvement was received;

10. Gain an idea about any significant losses experienced or are being experienced and how these were/are being coped with.

» It can present the service user with the opportunity to:

1. Talk about themselves;

2. Decide how much to disclose and what to withhold;

3. Take tentative, trusting steps or not;

4. Be truthful or deceitful.

In Chapter 1 I briefly mentioned Daniel Pelka. For reasons we do not fully understand, the parenting Daniel received was very different from that of his two siblings. When undertaking a personal history in a case of suspected child abuse and/or where such differences may be occurring, it can be instructive to ask how the parents felt about the pregnancies they'd had, the meaning the pregnancy held and what the baby meant or would mean (what portent he or she or it had). It is important to establish the identity of the biological parents of the children in the family and if these are different to the current carers. In Daniel's case he had a younger brother, who was a half-sibling and the biological child of Daniel's mother and her partner at the time of his death.

It may also be important to enquire as to the circumstances of the conception, ie if it was the result of violence or rape. These are difficult, intrusive and probing questions but if we are not prepared to address such issues we may not even get close to understanding *what is going on* in these thankfully uncommon, nonetheless tragic, cases.

There are other reasons why having an understanding of a personal history is important. The service user's experience of loss and its significance to them can be instructive. Life-story work can present an opportunity for a looked-after child to know the sequence of events and possibly reasons why they had frequent moves or a disrupted childhood and through this begin to come to terms with what happened. Similarly, reminiscence work with dementia sufferers can promote memory recall.

Another contribution from psycho-dynamic theory which I consider to be of significant importance is attachment. I would apply attachment theory to determine the attachment style the child or children appear to have to their primary caregivers. This involves observing their interaction, which can be instructive in its own right. Once an understanding of the attachment style which characterises the relationship is obtained, consideration can be given to how to encourage the characteristics of a secure attachment to a greater extent should this be necessary.

A further contribution from psycho-dynamic theory I would consider is what sort of internal working model my service user might have. The personal history may offer insights into this but it is important to come to an understanding of the service user's sense of self-concept and self-esteem. This may inform the sort of expectations the service user has and help the social worker establish where their service user 'is at'. If they were pretty much at *rock bottom*, some esteem work may be necessary before a strengths-based approach could be credibly undertaken.

Contributions from behaviourism

Behaviour modification through operant conditioning has a wide range of applications. It can feel as though the *operant* is manipulating the person whose behaviour is being modified which is, of course, the case, but this is fairly commonplace; advertising relies on it and if you have a loyalty card in your purse or wallet or you are now taking your own bags to the supermarket rather than buying their plastic ones, you too are subject to it. You might ameliorate the sense of being a manipulator by explaining how positive reinforcement works in modifying behaviour.

I have applied behaviour modification through operant conditioning in my work: in youth justice to prevent or curtail re-offending; with children, young people and their carers; and with children, young people and adults with learning disabilities. As theory goes it is quite transparent and intellectually accessible but can be used with those who lack capacity or whose capacity is impaired, in so far as they don't need to understand the methodology, unlike the case with CBT. There are some points to bear in mind when embarking on behaviour modification:

» Behaviour modification involves change and loss, things people do not usually readily engage with and prefer to avoid so some resistance is a normative response.

» Some behaviours are easier to change and lose than others so scope the change and loss involved: what is substituting for the losses?

» Keep the number of *behaviours to change* small.

» What support/rewards are being offered during the process of change?

» Ensure the positive reinforcements being used are really desired (ideally greater than what the behaviour marked for extinction means to the person).

» Be creative; praise itself can be a powerful positive reinforcement.

» Don't withdraw immediately after the point the behaviour changed as the period of early maintenance can be stressful and vulnerable to relapse.

» In family conflict behaviour modification can be used to bargain with and to strike deals.

In relation to the last point, I visited a family in response to a request by a parent to receive their teenage child into care. This wasn't a bluff; they had his bags packed and were more than prepared to sign any required papers. They said they had come to an *'irrevocable breakdown in their relationship'* and initially it only added to the sense of crisis when I refused to simply collect him and his belongings. Eventually they were prepared to write a list of respective complaints, although from separate rooms. The complaints on each list numbered more than 20. I left after three hours without the teenager but having reduced the items on the list to two each, having gained an agreement from the teenager to address the two remaining complaints of the parent and the parent to address the two remaining complaints of the teenager and a commitment from me to visit in a week to see how it had gone.

On another occasion I used a star chart as a vehicle for reinforcement with an eight-year-old boy whose mother was having difficulty managing his behaviour. I enquired a week later as to how this had gone, only to discover he had torn it up after day one! So a cautionary note when entrusting the management of the behaviour modification programme to someone: make sure they can administer it! It was, of course, the mum that needed work in managing her son's behaviour.

Conversation with service users drawing on what was disclosed through taking a personal history can provide additional insight as to the extent any learnt behaviour is being replicated (social learning theory) or if alternatives to the present circumstances cannot be envisaged (learned helplessness).

Wherever the presenting issues concern 'problem' behaviour, using the ABC analysis can be a useful inroad into *what's going on* and provides a vehicle with which to create alternatives. The service user can 'test out' alternative behaviours and their respective consequences.

Mentoring can provide a refreshingly different source of motivation, one in which the mentee can respect and seek to emulate their mentor. I have used mentors in my work with young offenders but also with young mums, where their mentor was a Home-Start volunteer who had been a young mum herself. I feel the use of mentors to be an underused, and largely untapped, motivational resource.

CBT has, I believe, a sound theoretical construct and giving consideration to the thoughts and feelings the service user associates with their behaviour can yield valuable insights. The skilled practitioner does not have to be trained as a CBT therapist in order to challenge an association between thoughts, feelings and the consequential behaviour where it is unhelpful to the function of the service user. The use of challenge can be powerful as shown in the example given in Chapter 2 in which creating cognitive dissonance was used to motivate change, but the use of challenge needs careful consideration as it often provokes a defensive reaction. Motivational interviewing seeks to promote engagement in change without challenging presenting behaviours.

Desensitisation techniques can be effective in addressing evasive behaviours that appear to be of phobic proportions and I have used it successfully with school refusers.

Contributions from systems theory

I cannot think of a situation in which the application of systems theory would not beneficially inform an analysis of that situation or contribute to its improvement. In fact I would go as far as to suggest that the failure to appreciate the social context, including the lack of one, in which people function would significantly impair the quality of any assessment and analysis of *what's going on*. In respect of social work with children and families, the importance of the social context is recognised in the baseline domain of the Assessment Framework: Family and Environmental Factors. In my work with children and their families it has been essential to establish who lives in the household, who visits the household and the roles they have in doing so. In addition to the contribution systems analysis has in information gathering and assessment, it can bring benefits to function when applied as an intervention. In a situation where the children in a family are in need, as per the S17 (10) definition in the Children Act 1989, an assessment would be made of the extent to which the primary caregivers meet their children's needs but this does not have to be restricted to what the caregivers can provide. The additional benefits of contact with extended family, of day care or nursery provision, of breakfast and afterschool clubs can make an invaluable contribution to the overall extent to which children's' needs are met.

In my work seeking to safeguard and promote the welfare of children and young people, I have looked to increase protective factors in their lives by seeking ways to develop their *ecomaps* or systems. I can recall a young girl who was assessed as being subject to emotional abuse and accordingly there was intensive work being undertaken with her caregivers; however, she loved horses and arranging initially volunteer work with a local stables that later led to a part-time job was hugely important to her and offered so much in terms of improving her self-concept and esteem.

Manipulating the systems and social capital people have access to can yield real improvements in the quality of people's lives. Conversely, a reduction of this through a significant loss, for example, can result in the recognised 'stages' of bereavement and existential crisis.

Contributions from radical theory

I have alluded to the uneasy relationship social work has with radical theory in Chapter 2 as to how the profession itself can be critiqued from a radical perspective, resulting in a charge that social work contributes to the very discrimination and oppression it so earnestly seeks to challenge. However, putting that argument aside, radical theory offers a critical analysis of how society functions and the extent to which it meets the needs of its members. At the time of writing the World Economic Forum was meeting in Davos and to concentrate minds about this event Oxfam published a claim that the combined wealth of eight men was greater than that of half the world's poorest population (*The Guardian*, 16 January 2017). It is difficult to disagree with the charity's comment that such a level of disparity was '*beyond grotesque*'. Extrapolating this to how the structural inequalities detrimentally affected the life chances of individual service users is complicated but a relationship undoubtedly exists; however, it seems to me that there is little that social work can do to address it. Social work does not exist outside of the society that gave rise to it and as such is a product of it. An individual social worker might choose to vote in a certain way or become politically active in their spare time but as for an effective intervention within traditional case-work, perhaps there is little more to do other than have an awareness of the impact structural inequality has on society and on the lives of service users.

A legitimate expression of radicalism as a social work intervention can be realised in community development work. I worked for a local authority as a community development worker in the 1980s. One initiative I played a part in was a *tops off* housing campaign which targeted a block of double-decked flats as part of the district council's housing stock. The flats were in a poor state of repair and considered *the end of the line* in terms of allocation. The local housing association, comprised of tenants, successfully campaigned to have the top deck removed and the ground floor flats converted to terraced houses complete with a small front garden, and the removal of a communal grassed area. The community development worker's role was to help facilitate the functioning of the campaign's committee which was formed for the purpose. Today there are few such posts and those that there are tend to be outside of local government.

A radical analysis can make an important critical contribution to understanding the dynamic of power relationships. Feminism for example has opened up a whole discourse on how women and men relate to each other and speaks specifically to certain issues, for example, domestic abuse, child sexual exploitation and teenage relationships. These and similar issues that involve the abuse of power within interpersonal relationships are often subject to statutory social work intervention and a social worker needs an intellectual appreciation of radical theory to be able to come to an understanding of the context in which such behaviour takes place.

Contributions from the approaches selected

Strengths-based approaches

I cannot conceive of a social work intervention in which a strengths-based approach would not bring benefits for the recipients. Simply the recognition of what is currently being achieved, sometimes in stressful, difficult circumstances, can boost esteem and bolster resilience. Some formatted intervention systems such as Signs of Safety structure the approach into its method; one of the opening questions being '*what's working well?*' Of course, in situations where this is quite limited one would need to be measured less they appear *Pollyanna-like* but we know from the humanistic approach that the social worker needs to be 'congruent', which provides a safeguard from being overly optimistic. However, there can be few situations in which a modicum of praise and encouragement, or making confidence and capability-building comments would be inappropriate or produce negative outcomes.

Existential approaches

As I would describe myself as an existentialist, I feel comfortable with this approach and it holds no fear for me. This cannot be assumed in respect of the service user who may find the prospect of taking responsibly for themselves challenging or even threatening as it confers change and has philosophical consequences for one's notion of being. However, one does not need to become an existentialist to benefit from an existentially orientated approach. The primary advantage of such an approach could be the liberation from predestined outcomes. The origin of the predestination has to be identified and the transfer of power from 'it' to the person acceptable. All well and good where the *pre-destination* comes from dysfunctional family tradition: '*we've always done it that way*'. Inviting the service user to take command of the bridge and steer a different course may be acceptable. However, consider the situation where the person believes the origin of the pre-destination to be the will of their god, or their fate or linked to their sense of identity or salvation. They are unlikely to counten-ance the transfer of power and responsibility existentialism requires; it may even be oppressive to ask them; and so the potency of existentialism is limited as a force for change when confronted with a strong sense of faith or destiny.

Humanistic approaches

Humanistic approaches in relation to social work are best defined by the skill set that identifies them. It may help the practitioner's sense of authenticity and congruence if they are humanists but it is not a prerequisite; as with existentialism, one does not have to be a humanist to benefit from a humanistic approach. The principles behind the skills employed in working in a person-centred way can be considered to be of uni-versal application in any professional helping relationship. Furthermore, their effect-iveness is not dependent on the recipient being a humanist themselves as they appeal to all of humanity.

Problem-solving approaches

The appeal of problem-solving approaches for both practitioners and service users is evident in the transparency and openness that characterise it. There is nothing in the intervention going on at a *subconscious* level and the approach is dismissive of the clutter of the past. While these may be considered advantageous, they are, of course, the 'Achilles heel' of the approach for if there are psycho-social log jams preventing change and progress, a solely problem-solving approach is unlikely to be successful. That said, a problem-solving approach can bring a refreshing pragmatism to an intervention in which both the practitioner and service user can see the end to. The use of written agreements can introduce a quasi-contractual element to the working relationship which, if done well, conveys a mutual endeavour promoting partnership working. However, in safeguarding work in which the stakes are high, the potential for it to be seen as a coercive tool should be acknowledged and refuted as the written agreement should be concerned with bringing about an improvement in the lives of the children it relates to.

And what about the case study...?

Well, this would depend on what works for you and what you think may work for Annette and Andy. If you are a practitioner it is likely you will have established your preferences for the theories and approaches you like to work with. If you are a student you will be trying some out on your placements and beginning to have preferences, but in any event I would encourage you to be adventurous and creative as there is a rich pallette from which to select colours for your picture.

As for what worked for me, were I the social worker to Annette, Andy, Sam and Ben, I would use an initial visit for introductions and explain what my intervention may mean for them, including what the assessment I would be undertaking would involve and to gain an idea of their expectations and concerns. I would work in a person-centred way to the best of my ability. On a subsequent visit I would take a personal history to express interest, gain information and insight and a key for motivation as previously discussed.

I would be interested in gaining some idea of Annette and Andy's internal working model. I would observe and assess attachment styles between them and the children and discuss why this was important. I would recognise strengths as appropriate, including the structure available through the Signs of Safety method if franchised to the authority and adopt problem-solving techniques supported by behaviour modification for issues that lend themselves to this, such as the rubbish in the home and the 'open door' policy. I would consider the use of a written agreement for some of these issues, including any drug use and its management.

I would be interested in Annette and Andy's social network and sources of support and seek to establish if they were content with these or if additional support was necessary. I may seek to test out if Annette thought a befriender from Home-Start or similar could make a useful contribution. If there was a suggestion of having to 'plough the same furrow' as the past or follow some predestined course, I may challenge this through an existential approach. It may be appropriate to address other associations between thoughts, feelings and behaviours that presented obstacles using CBT. There may be a remit to address some presenting difficulty in the relationship between Annette and Andy if this impacted on the welfare of the children. If Annette or Andy's finances were adversely affected through the use of pay-day loan firms, it may be useful to introduce the idea of a credit union as a less exploitative resource.

Can we find the right combination of theory, approach and method of intervention to guarantee successful intervention?

If such a combination exists it is unlikely that it will be apparent. It would not be ethical to 're-run' an intervention in the hope of discovering it. Furthermore, it would not be possible to return to the same place prior to an intervention having taken place as some change will have occurred. So, this quest is unattainable in any absolute sense. However, accurate and appropriate information gathering can lead to a good assessment from which an insightful analysis can result in a plan of intervention which optimised the likelihood of a successful intervention. We may never be able to gain an exact picture of what's going on but this fortunately is not a prerequisite for intervention to be effective.

Consider Simon, who is 13 and has come to the attention of children's services through poor school attendance.

What's (really) going on?

Simon's dad suffers with depression; his mum has MS. The 'needs' of the parents are significant and woven into the family's function in which Simon has come to play a significant part, almost to the point of dependency. Simon has, for some considerable time, been receiving subliminal messages reinforcing this and has come to the point whereby he worries about this parents when he is not there.

Simon's situation could be responded to in a number of ways:

> » He could be assessed as a young carer to his parents.

> » Using systems theory, family therapy could be applied.

» Direct work with the parents could be undertaken.

» Provision of services to the parents could be made.

» Direct work with Simon could be undertaken, including looking at early separation, associated anxiety (psycho-dynamic), reintegration to school, desensitisation, CBT, behaviour modification or the use of a mentor.

So, quite different responses could be made, all of which could result in some improvement in Simon's school attendance. Although it may not be necessary to 'get to the bottom' of *what's going on* in order to bring about some improvement in Simon's school attendance, the intervention could be 'bespoke' to the situation if an understanding of it was sufficiently close. This highlights the importance that a good assessment and accurate analysis play in planning intervention.

The only requirement for intervention to be effective is that it works for the practitioner and service user. Identifying what combination of theory, approach and method of intervention is appropriate and likely to render intervention 'effective' is, of course, down to the skill and craft of the practitioner, and elements of the social worker's experience and their 'practice wisdom' contribute to the mix; but these, at first glance, abstract, notions are dependent on the quality of the practitioner's reflection and critical analysis.

Reflection and critical analysis

The 'preferences' the practitioner may have developed for particular theories, approaches and their respective methods of intervention will be informed by their knowledge of them and their skill in applying them, but also to some extent, influenced by their experience of using them. There are theoretical models to use when reflecting on practice, a well-known one being Kolb's experiential learning cycle. This model takes the practitioner through the stages of hypothesis, intervention, outcome and reflection on outcome. However, at its simplest, reflection and critical analysis is concerned with learning from experience.

Do we learn from experience? Experience provides us with the opportunity to learn from it but doing so is not an automatic process. Learning from experience is a deliberate, conscious act that requires intention, time and some energy dedicating to it if it is to be learnt from. Let's be honest; we cannot always muster the resources necessary – where this is the case we do not learn from experience, which exposes us to the possibility of repeating the same behaviour irrespective of the previous outcome.

What must be present for reflection and critical analysis to take place?

»　A willingness to do so must be present.

»　The ability to do so must be present, the cognitive ability to *think it through*.

»　An experience that is amenable to learn from must also be present.

»　A working environment that promotes it – a learning environment – that allows the practitioner to 'stand back' from the 'coal face' of practice to *perspective take* and undertake some analysis of an intervention.

Sources of information for reflection and critical analysis

Although the practitioner is the most important source of information for reflection and critical analysis, why limit it to one source? Why not ask the service user when evaluating the intervention '*what, out of the work we have done together, worked well for you?*' It might not be appropriate to wait to evaluate the intervention to obtain such information. In circumstances where the intervention was clearly not working, it would be pertinent to reflect *in* practice, during the intervention rather than delay to reflect *on* practice. Another significant source of information is from the practice supervisor, assuming a healthy working relationship exists, in which the practitioner values their supervisor's perspective. There may be other appropriate sources from which to obtain additional information, such as a practitioner with whom you have co-worked the intervention. Finally, when reflecting on your intervention do factor in 'affect'. What was happening for you at the time? How did you feel about the intervention and those involved? Neglecting the potential influence of this *affective dimension* could result in a flawed analysis.

Optimising your use of theories, approaches and their methods of intervention

A part of being able to take pride in your practice and fulfilling the Kantian duty to provide your service user with the best service you can is dependent on your ability to optimise your use of theories, approaches and apply their methods of intervention with confidence. Consequently, it is important that the variety of theories and approaches you use or your confidence in their application is not limited or undermined simply through lack of knowledge or skill, or rejected through early negative experience rather than through sound critical reflection. So, you are encouraged to be bold and creative in your use of theories and approaches in your practice and to be mindful that different theories and approaches may work differently with different people so remain open to ideas and to learning.

I will conclude this chapter by recalling some casework I was involved in, while on placement during my course of qualification, which concerned a family with five young children. The children were, to various extents, considered to have developmental delay. Causation through learning disability was dismissed following appropriate assessment and attention turned towards the quality of stimulation in the home environment. Their mum could not have anything 'out of place'. I once observed her partner combing the frill of a carpet straight again after having been rucked through footfall. It's fine to be fastidious about such things but with five young children it was problematic, their solution being few toys, no mess or clutter and inappropriate restriction of movement of the children. A psychologist was assigned to help work with the family who concluded that the mum's intolerance to anything out of place was linked to her need to impose structure and control in reaction to the death of her father in her late childhood. I will admit that making a connection with the need for bereavement work in response to the presenting problems was far from my mind but I came to have some respect for this analysis.

The point in recalling this is to illustrate the need to be open to accommodating ideas. We may be sceptical about certain ideas; we may fail to select the theory or approach or combination thereof that could have optimised the success of an intervention. However, we should avoid being dismissive of ideas on account of prejudice. We are not dealing with the equations of an exact science but the art of living and our practice needs to reflect this.

References

Children Act 1989 (c.41). London: TSO. [online] Available at: www.legislation.gov.uk/ukpga/1989/41/contents (accessed 24 March 2017).

Goldring, M (2017) Eight men own more than 3.6 billion people do: our economics is broken. *The Guardian*, 16 January. [online] Available at: www.theguardian.com/commentisfree/2017/jan/16/eight-people-earn-more-billion-economics-broken (accessed 16 January 2017).

Kolb, D (2015) *Experiential Learning: Experience as the Source of Learning and Development* (2nd ed). Upper Saddle River, New Jersey: Prentice Hall.

Signs of Safety (2015) *Signs of Safety*. Perth, Australia: Resolutions Consultancy. [online] Available at: www.signsofsafety.net/signs-of-safety-2/ (accessed 24 March 2017).

Chapter 5 | Conclusion

Well, what did you make of all that?

Undoubtedly there is a rich array of diverse, even contradictory, explanations and approaches with which to consider the equally rich array of human behaviour. The analysis offered by a psycho-dynamic explanation of human behaviour is complex and challenging. I am mindful of the feminist critique of Freud's family drama which suggests that his 'patients' were simply recounting their experience of childhood sexual abuse. You can understand the appeal of problem-solving approaches by comparison. Psycho-dynamic analysis cannot claim to be 'user-friendly' as it is highly deterministic and largely inaccessible without expert interpretation. It could be criticised for being a self-perpetuating industry. One can imagine a Woody Allen style sketch in which Woody Allen says to his psychotherapist '*Gee, I've been coming to see you for years now and I'm not sure if anything has changed*', to which the psychotherapist replies, '*Do you want to talk about this?*' But can it be disregarded as implied by a radical analysis and some of the approaches we have considered? Can we simply dispense with our past? I doubt it. Suppose there really was something in it; suppose our early experiences create circuitry in our developing brains that seeds personality traits and behaviours that require the level of unpicking implied in psychotherapy. If this were the case, all that which has been discussed, with the exception of psycho-dynamic theory, may be well-intended and in part even helpful but condemned to address the symptoms rather than the cause. Despite finding this quite a scary thought I find I cannot dismiss it. One only has to look at recidivism rates for offending to know there is something going on that interferes with the ability to behave rationally. Although psychoanalysis as an intervention is not available to the social worker without additional relevant training, an analysis of attachment styles and consideration of how it may contribute to one's internal working model are within a qualified social worker's range of skills and are significant factors in any assessment in working with children and families.

It is undeniable that behaviourism works. We can actually see it working. Consider the mass behaviour modification exercise that has taken place via operant conditioning when supermarkets started charging for plastic bags. Despite this only being 5 pence it has resulted in shoppers taking their own reusable bags when they go shopping.

CBT is undoubtedly a powerful tool to bring about a change in behaviour. It can even produce significant results when applied vicariously; the tragic death of Jade Goody prompted many young women to go and have a test for cervical cancer.

The part *systems* play in the functioning and quality of our lives seems fundamental to our existence; they give us our context

The optimistic and life-affirming stance of the approaches we have considered has to be beneficial. The human potential for healing, personal growth and development seems to be an attribute of the species that with a little nourishment can flourish. However, radical theory tells us that people need to be dealt a playable hand if they are to participate in society and serves to remind us that well-being cannot be disassociated from just levels of equality.

Ready to apply your knowledge and skills?

I have been in the process of becoming a social worker throughout the duration of my practising career. There have been times when segments of this process appear to have been concluded – for example, upon finishing my initial and post-qualifying studies, but any notion of the process having come to an end is an illusion; it is a career-long process. So it is difficult to know when you are sufficiently 'tooled-up' to use the theories and approaches and to apply their methods of intervention with any precision. We want to offer our service users a greater degree of confidence in our ability than well-intended trial and error. This is why it is incumbent upon us to give thought to the range of models and methods available and to become skilled in utilising those we want to work with. A degree of trial and error during the period over which we develop competence and confidence is inevitable. There is no shortcut in learning our craft but I would encourage the student or inexperienced practitioner to try out different theories and approaches as it is only by doing so that you will become proficient in their use.

Using the '*conscious competence*' (Howell, 1982, pp 29–33) model may provide a tool you can use to assess when you are ready to 'road test' a theory, approach and its method of intervention.

There are four stages in this model: unconscious incompetence; conscious incompetence; conscious competence and unconscious competence. Reference to the process of learning to drive will be used to illustrate the stages.

1. Unconscious incompetence: describes the state prior to starting to learn to drive in that *the driver to be* is unaware of lacking the skills they need to drive.

2. Conscious incompetence: here, the learner driver is having their first lesson and really struggling to co-ordinate the multiple tasks involved in moving off, mirror, signal, throttle, clutch control etc. They are all too aware of lacking competence in co-ordinating these skills.

3. Conscious competence: it's the day of their driving test. They have acquired the skills required to drive but they are mindful and vigilant in exercising them.

4. Unconscious competence: the driver is now experienced and can undertake a journey without conscious regard of the skills required to do so.

The same model can be applied to the acquisition of knowledge of theories, approaches and the skills required to apply them.

Prior to learning anything about social science and these ideas about human behaviour, you are unaware of what you need to have in order to come to an informed view.

After the first lecture on theories and methods, you may feel somewhat daunted by what you'll have to get to grips with to feel as though you have an understanding of this topic. You're aware you will need to study this and read around the subject in addition to attending the module's lectures and seminars in order to grasp the material.

You have completed the module on theories and methods and passed the assessment of your understanding of it. You are on placement in a *looked-after* children's team and your practice educator is discussing the life-story work you are doing with Sophie during supervision. You are reflecting on the number of placement moves Sophie has had and the consequential losses she has experienced as a result. From the conversations you have had with her it was apparent that she has interpreted some of these moves as a rejection of her, and you have considered what impact this has had for her attachments and internal working model.

You are now an advanced practitioner and find you don't have to 'think everything through' as you did when newly qualified in your first few years of practice. You feel you can read and sum up a situation quite quickly.

The exercise of 'practice wisdom' is one of the advantages of being an experienced practitioner but I would guard against describing a role for 'intuition' in social work practice. There is a danger in moving from conscious competence to unconscious competence as the social worker needs to be accountable for their practice and subject it to reflection and critical analysis. Furthermore, a student shadowing or being supervised would gain little from the experience if the worker failed to offer a rationale for their practice.

Final thoughts

The most important thing the theories, approaches and their respective methods of intervention offer the social work practitioner is a systematic framework through which they can set about their occupational task. This enables them to come to an understanding of *what's going on* and offers an organised approach to doing something about it.

What you bring to the situation, the combination of knowledge, skills and values you have, your interpersonal skills and how you convey this matters, the outcome matters and the quality of the service user's life matters, and constructs the stage upon which your intervention will be played out. The quality of the relationship you build with your service user will be a significant, if not crucial, indicator in predicting the outcome of an intervention. However, the appropriate and effective use of theory, approach and their methods of intervention will direct the intervention and be fundamental to its outcome.

May I take this opportunity to wish you well with both endeavours.

Reference

Howell, W (1982) *The Empathic Communicator*. Belmont, MA: Wadsworth Publishing Company.

References and further reading

Alexander, C (1850) *Hymns for Little Children*. Philadelphia, USA: Herman Hooker.

Bailey, R and Brake, M (1975) *Radical Social Work*. London: Edward Arnold.

BBC News (2012) Raoul Moat victim PC David Rathband found dead at home. [online] Available at: www.bbc.co.uk/news/uk-england-tyne-17216389 (accessed 24 March 2017).147

BBC News (2016) Bailey Gwynne death: Pupil stabbing death was 'avoidable'. [online] Available at: www.bbc.co.uk/news/uk-scotland-north-east-orkney-shetland-37606361 (accessed 20 February 2017).

Beckett, C and Horner, N (2015) *Essential Theory for Social Work Practice*. London: Sage.

Blandin, J and Machin, S (2007) *Recent Changes in Intergenerational Mobility in Britain*. London: Sutton Trust. [online] Available at: http://cep.lse.ac.uk/pubs/download/special/Recent_Changes_in_Intergenerational_Mobility_in_Britain.pdf (accessed 23 March 2017).

Brief Family Therapy Center (2007) *Solutions since 1982*. Milwaukee, USA: Brief Family Therapy Center. [online] Available at: www.sfbta.org/bftc/steve_de_shazer_insoo_kim_burg.html (accessed 24 March 2017).

British Association of Social Workers (BASW) (2012) *The Code of Ethics for Social Work: Statement of Principles*. Birmingham: British Association of Social Workers. [online] Available at: http://cdn.basw.co.uk/upload/basw_95243-9.pdf (accessed 24 March 2017).

British Association of Social Workers (BASW) (2015) *Professional Capabilities Framework*. Birmingham: BASW. [online] Available at: www.basw.co.uk/pcf/ (accessed 18 March 2017).

Care Act 2014 (c.23) (2014) London: TSO. [online] Available at: www.legislation.gov.uk/ukpga/2014/23/contents/enacted (accessed 23 March 2017).

Casement, P (2014) *On Learning from the Patient* (2nd ed). Abingdon: Routledge.

Children Act 1989 (c.41). London: TSO. [online] Available at: www.legislation.gov.uk/ukpga/1989/41/contents (accessed 20 February 2017).

Children and Families Act 2014 (c.6) (2014) London: TSO. [online] Available at: www.legislation.gov.uk/ukpga/2014/6/contents/enacted (accessed 18 March 2017).

Children, Young Persons, and Their Families Act 1989 (1989) Wellington, New Zealand: Parliamentary Counsel Office. [online] Available at: www.legislation.govt.nz/act/public/1989/0024/latest/DLM147088.html (accessed 23 March 2017).

Crawford, K and Walker, J (2014) *Social Work and Human Development*. London: Learning Matters.

Daniel, B (2003) The Value of Resilience as a Concept for Practice in Residential Settings. *Scottish Journal of Residential Child Care*, 2(1): 6–15. [online] Available at: www.researchgate.net/profile/Brigid_Daniel/publication/264878107_The_Value_of_Resilience_as_a_Concept_for_Practice_in_Residential_Settings/links/55e95bb008aeb65162647b72.pdf (accessed 20 February 2017).

Davies, C (2015) Number of suicides in UK increases, with male rate highest since 2001. *The Guardian*, 19 February. [online] Available at: www.theguardian.com/society/2015/feb/19/number-of-suicides-uk-increases-2013-male-rate-highest-2001 (accessed 24 March 2017).

Department for Education (2015) *Knowledge and Skills Statements for Child and Family Social Work*. Manchester: Department for Education. [online] Available at: www.gov.uk/government/publications/knowledge-and-skills-statements-for-child-and-family-social-work (accessed 18 March 2017).

Doran, G (1981) There's a S.M.A.R.T. Way to Write Management's Goals and Objectives. *Management Review*, 70(11): 35–6.

Ferguson, I and Woodward, R (2009) *Radical Social Work in Practice*. Bristol: Policy Press.

Goldring, M (2017) Eight men own more than 3.6 billion people do: our economics is broken. *The Guardian*, 16 January. [online] Available at: www.theguardian.com/commentisfree/2017/jan/16/eight-people-earn-more-billion-economics-broken (accessed 16 January 2017).

Harris, R (2002) As Macmillan never said: that's enough quotations. *The Telegraph*, 4 June. [online] Available at: swww.telegraph.co.uk/comment/personal-view/3577416/As-Macmillan-never-said-thats-enough-quotations.html (accessed 24 March 2017).

Healy, K (2005) *Social Work Theories in Context*. Basingstoke: Palgrave Macmillan.

Healy, K (2014) *Social Work Theories in Context Creating Frameworks for Practice*. Basingstoke: Palgrave Macmillan.

Hogarth, W (1751) *Gin Lane*. London: Tate. [online] Available at: www.tate.org.uk/art/artworks/hogarth-gin-lane-t01799 (accessed 18 March 2017).

Howe, D (2009) *A Brief Introduction to Social Work Theory*. Basingstoke: Palgrave Macmillan.

Howe, D (2013) *Empathy: What It Is and Why It Matters*. Basingstoke: Palgrave Macmillan.

Howe, D, Brandon, M, Hinings, D and Schofield, G (1999) *Attachment Theory, Child Maltreatment and Family Support*. Palgrave: Basingstoke.

Howell, W (1982) *The Empathic Communicator*. Belmont, MA: Wadsworth Publishing Company.

Human Rights Act 1998 (c.42). London: TSO. [online] Available at: www.legislation.gov.uk/ukpga/1998/42/contents (accessed 24 March 2017).

International Federation of Social Workers (IFSW) (2014) Global definition of social work. Berne, Switzerland: IFSW. [online] Available at: http://ifsw.org/get-involved/global-definition-of-social-work/ (accessed 18 March 2017).

James, O (2016) *Not in Your Genes*. Vermilion: London.

Kolb, D (2015) *Experiential Learning: Experience as the Source of Learning and Development* (2nd ed). Upper Saddle River, New Jersey: Prentice Hall.

Kubler-Ross, E (1969) *On Death and Dying*. London: Routledge.

Lavalette, M (ed) (2011) *Radical Social Work Today*. Bristol: Policy Press.

Maclean, S and Harrison, R (2008) *Social Work Theory: A Straightforward Guide for Practice Assessors and Placement Supervisors*. Rugeley: Kirwin Maclean Associates Ltd.

Marsh, P and Doel, M (2005) *The Task-centred Book*. Abingdon: Routledge.

Mearns, D and Thorne, B (2007) *Person-Centred Counselling in Action* (3rd ed). London: Sage.

Morgan, N (2016) *Children's Social Care Reform: Written Statement*. Manchester: Department for Education. [online] Available at: www.parliament.uk/business/publications/written-questions-answers-statements/written-statement/Commons/2016-01-14/HCWS469/ (accessed 20 February 2017).

Munch, E (1893) *The Scream*. Oslo, Norway: Eduard Munch.org. [online] Available at: www.edvardmunch.org/the-scream.jsp (accessed 24 March 2017).

Munro, E (2010) *The Munro Review of Child Protection*. Manchester: Department for Education. [online] Available at: www.gov.uk/government/uploads/system/uploads/attachment_data/file/175407/The MunroReview-Part_one.pdf (accessed 23 March 2017).

Murray Parkes, C (1998) *Coping with Loss*. Oxford: John Wiley.145

Parrish, M (2010) *Social Work Perspectives on Human Behaviour*. Maidenhead: Open University Press.

Parrish, M (2014) *Social Work Perspectives on Human Behaviour* (2nd ed). Maidenhead: Open University Press.

Parsons, T (1991) *Social System*. London: Routledge.

Payne, M (2005) *Modern Social Work Theory* (3rd ed). Basingstoke: Palgrave Macmillan.

Payne, M (2011) *Humanistic Social Work: Core Principles in Practice*. Basingstoke: Palgrave Macmillan.

Perlman, H (1957) *Social Casework: A Problem-solving Process*. Chicago: Chicago University Press.

Perry, B (2001) Curiosity: The Fuel of Development. *Early Childhood Development Today*, 15(6): 22–4.

Pringle, M L K, Great Britain Department of Health and Social Security, National Childrens Bureau (1986) *The Needs of Children: A Personal Perspective*, 3rd ed. London: Hutchinson.

Reid, W and Epstein, L (1972) *Task-Centred Casework*. New York: Columbia University Press.

Rogers, C (1961) *On Becoming a Person*. Boston: Houghton Mifflin Publishers.

Ruch, G, Turney, D and Ward, A (2010) *Relationship-based Social Work*. London: Jessica Kingsley Publishers.

Saleebey, D (2002) Introduction: Power in the People, in Saleebey, D (ed) *The Strengths Perspective in Social Work Practice* (3rd ed). Boston: Allyn and Bacon, pp 1–22.

Saleebey, D (2009) *Strengths Perspective in Social Work* (5th ed). Boston: Pearson.

Saleebey, D (2012) *The Strengths Perspective in Social Work Practice* (6th ed). Cambridge: Pearson.

Sartre, J P (2002) *Existentialism and Human Emotions*. New York: Citadel Press.

Signs of Safety (2015) *Signs of Safety*. Perth, Australia: Resolutions Consultancy. [online] Available at: www.signsofsafety.net/signs-of-safety-2/ (accessed 24 March 2017).

Skynner, R and Cleese, J (1984) *Families and How to Survive Them*. London: Mandarin.

Smale, G, Tuson, G, Staham, D and Campling, J (2000) *Social Work and Social Problems: Working towards Social Inclusion and Social Change*. London: Palgrave Macmillan.

Stacey, K (2014) The real story of the miners' strike in five questions [blog], 3 January. [online] Available at: http://blogs.ft.com/westminster/2014/01/the-real-story-of-the-miners-strike-in-five-questions/ (accessed 23 March 2017).

Sutton, C (2006) *Helping Families with Troubled Children: A Preventative Approach* (2nd ed). Oxford: Wiley.

Sylva, K and Lunt, I (1989) *Child Development: A First Course*. Oxford: Blackwell.

Teater, B (2014) *An Introduction to Applying Social Work Theories and Methods*. Maidenhead: Open University Press; McGraw Hill Education.

Thompson, N (1992) *Existentialism and Social Work*. Aldershot: Avebury.

Thompson, N (2010) *Theorizing Social Work Practice*. Basingstoke: Palgrave Macmillan.

Turbett, C (2014) *Doing Radical Social Work*. Basingstoke: Palgrave Macmillan.

Turnell, A and Edwards, S (1997) Aspiring to Partnership: The Signs of Safety Approach to Child Protection. *Child Abuse Review*, 6(3): 179–90.

Turnell, A and Murphy, T (2014) *Signs of Safety Comprehensive Briefing Paper* (3rd ed). Perth, Australia: Resolutions Consultancy Pty Ltd.

Williams, C and Garland, A (2002) A Cognitive-Behavioural Therapy Assessment Model for Use in Everyday Clinical Practice. *Advances in Psychiatric Treatment*, 8: 172–9.

Worthington, D (2014) Looking back on the three day week. London: New Historian. [online] Available at: www.newhistorian.com/looking-back-three-day-week/2405/ (accessed 23 March 2017).

Wright, J (1768) *An Experiment on a Bird in the Air Pump*. London: National Gallery. [online] Available at: www.nationalgallery.org.uk/paintings/joseph-wright-of-derby-an-experiment-on-a-bird-in-the-air-pump (accessed 18 March 2017).

Index